P9-DDP-782

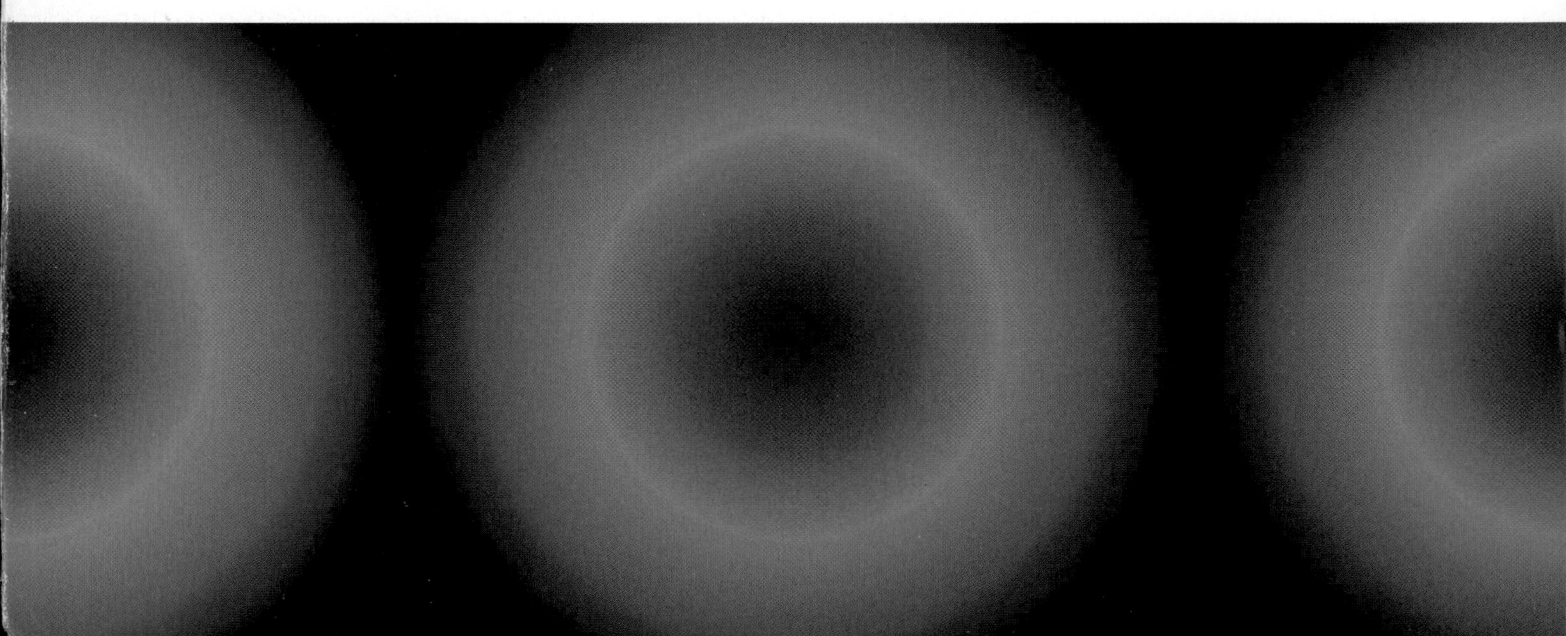

# Making the Band

by O-TOWN with K.M. Squires

Pocket Books

NEW YORK LONDON TORONTO SYDNEY SINGAPORE

An *Original* Publication of MTV Books/Pocket Books

POCKET BOOKS, a division of Simon & Schuster, Inc.
1230 Avenue of the Americas, New York, NY 10020



J Records
New York, NY

Trans Continental Records
7380 Sand Lake Road, Suite 350, Orlando, FL 32819

Exclusive Representation: Louis J. Pearlman
Trans Continental Management: MIke Cronin, Mike Morin
Management Representative: Joel Schaller
Booking Agency: Evolution Talent Agency, Craig Bruck
1776 Broadway, 15th Floor, New York, NY 10019
(212) 554-0300



ISBN: 0-7434-1701-1

First MTV Books/Pocket Books trade paperback printing December 2000

10 9 8 7 6 5 4 3 2 1



Cover photo: Ben Van Hook

Back cover photo: Walt Disney Parks and Resorts 2000 / Mark Ashman

Cover and interior design by pink design, inc. (www.pinkdesigninc.com)

Printed in the U.S.A.

*For John R. Squires and Elizabeth Marie Squires,*
*with much love*

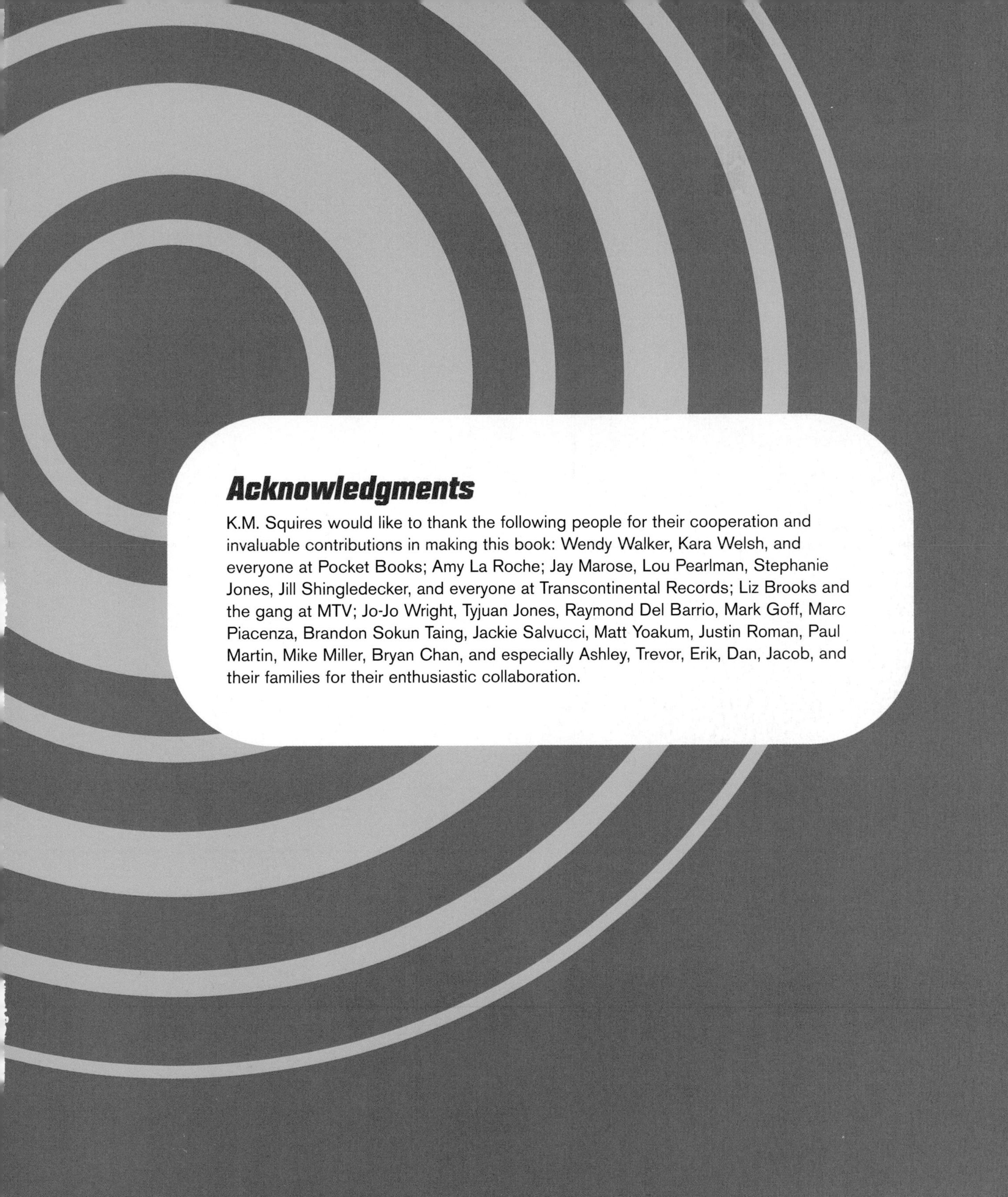


## Acknowledgments

K.M. Squires would like to thank the following people for their cooperation and invaluable contributions in making this book: Wendy Walker, Kara Welsh, and everyone at Pocket Books; Amy La Roche; Jay Marose, Lou Pearlman, Stephanie Jones, Jill Shingledecker, and everyone at Transcontinental Records; Liz Brooks and the gang at MTV; Jo-Jo Wright, Tyjuan Jones, Raymond Del Barrio, Mark Goff, Marc Piacenza, Brandon Sokun Taing, Jackie Salvucci, Matt Yoakum, Justin Roman, Paul Martin, Mike Miller, Bryan Chan, and especially Ashley, Trevor, Erik, Dan, Jacob, and their families for their enthusiastic collaboration.

Walt Disney Parks and Resorts 2000 / Mark Ashman

O-TOWN™

# Contents

This real-life series follows eight young performers as they compete for five positions in a new band. There are no actors and no scripts—just raw talent, a dream, and cameras recording every step of the journey.

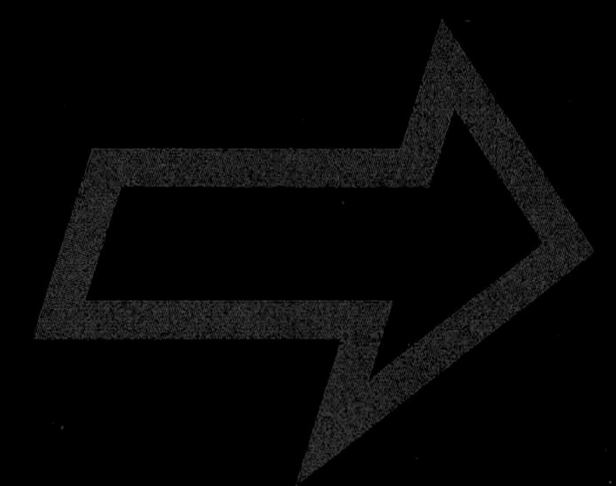

# Part One

# Making

©2000 ABC, Inc / Scott Garfield

# the Band

Ben Van Hook

# How to Make a Boy Band

## Lou Pearlman, record executive

Ken Mok of MTV asked me if I wanted to participate in a program about the genesis of making a boy band. Being that I have experience already with helping develop groups like the Backstreet Boys and 'N Sync, they thought I'd be the right guy.

In the beginning I was a little doubtful whether or not something like that could be a TV show. I asked them how they planned on doing it, and they told me it would be like *The Real World*, and that they would use the actual *Real World* production team, Bunim and Murray. Cameras would follow us through the whole process, documenting on a grand scale what I had already done in the past. I thought it sounded like a great idea.

It was such a great idea that we thought we should pitch it to a major network instead of putting it on MTV to reach a broader audience. It turned out that all the networks wanted it.

I remember pitching it to ABC, where it eventually ended up. There were two executives in the room hearing us out. They said, "Do you have any scripts?"

We answered, "It's unscripted."

They asked, "Do you have a pilot?"

We said, "We can't give you a pilot. We haven't shot the show yet."

They said, "Wait a minute—no script, no pilot. And you want us to take how many shows?"

"A whole season of thirteen," we responded, and they looked at us like we were out of our minds. But then finally they said, "Okay, we'll take it." Just like that. I was shocked. We got twenty-two shows out of it.

Lou Pearlman, maker of boy bands

Though I had developed boy bands before, the process of making O-Town was different than putting together the Backstreet Boys and 'N Sync. Those groups came from a local talent pool who more or less knew each other. For O-Town, we did a nationwide talent search, and the final five were complete strangers. O-Town used the same vocal coach and choreographers as other groups I worked with, but they had an accelerated time frame to make it work. I never, ever did it this quickly before.

We started the nationwide search by putting ads on MTV and on the Internet, and held the auditions in eight cities: Honolulu, Los Angeles, Las Vegas, Dallas, Nashville, Chicago, New York, and Orlando. To judge the hopefuls, we had help from MTV VJs, radio disc jockeys, talent agents, actors, actresses, singers, dancers, and our in-house core of judges from

Transcontinental Records. There were about fifty people total involved in the selection process.

Singing was the most important skill we were looking for. Dancing was the second thing. The guys with high marks in those areas were then interviewed by a psychologist, to learn about their backgrounds and see if they met the psychological standards necessary for the process of being filmed. Then the production team videotaped more interviews, where they drew out the guys' personalities, and considered how they looked on camera.

We chose twenty-five to come to Orlando and "compete" for eight spots, which were eventually whittled down to the final five.

## Jay Marose, publicist

The entire time I worked with bands, whether it was Take 5 or C Note or whomever, I got to know them, and part of what I do is try to learn who they are, not who they try to show. The television show was a way to show not only the image but also who these guys really are. By turning the cameras on, it would be impossible for anyone to say they were being anything other than themselves. That's an opportunity no band could possibly pass up.

During the auditioning process, the guys, unbeknownst to them, were being watched from the second they walked in. Some of us were pretending to be roadies, setting up tables, and getting everyone registered. We were watching them undercover, so to speak.

There were a couple of people in particular that stood out before we even spoke to them. Erik-Michael Estrada was standing in the crowd of three hundred and fifty kids and you couldn't take your eyes off of him—I don't know why. I think he was interviewing us as much as we were interviewing him. He was very introspective, looking at everything and trying to figure out what was going on. When he finished his interview we were already talking about how he would look in the band.

Ashley Angel was like that, too. He walked in with his guitar, and he was so engaging and friendly with the Bunim/Murray staff that I actually had a little debate with them about whether or not he was acting. They said, "He's an actor, he's acting," and I said, "I don't think he is." He was the last person we told who was going to make it, and I walked outside to get him. He was sitting by the pool, playing guitar, and completely oblivious to everything else around him. I told him it was time to go back inside, and he was like, "Just a second. I want to finish this song."

We saw about 1,800 auditions total, in all eight cities, and it was amazing: in each city we would all compare notes, and we all picked the same people.

One of the hundreds, learning the tryout songs at a listening station.

Aiming for the stars...another hopeful who didn't make it.

## Jo Jo Wright, disc jockey, KISS FM, Los Angeles

Lou Pearlman called me up and asked me if I wanted to be a judge. It sounded like a lot of fun, and I was curious to see what kind of talent was out there, and how these auditions were run. We were asked to rate the hopefuls on a scale from one to ten, for appearance, vocals, and dancing.

What really grabbed me is there are a lot of people out there who just cannot sing, so when somebody *could* sing, he really got my attention. There were also a few instances where the voice wasn't extra special but there was something else about that person, too, like a great presence, or a great soul.

One guy showed up who was probably sixty years old! He grabbed the mike and he started singing this song, and nobody knew what it was. When he got to the end of it he said: "I wrote that." And I thought, *Dude, you are cool!* He was like some old blues singer guy. Of course, he didn't make it. But he still sticks in my head.

The whole experience showed me that making a boy band is hard work. For Lou, I imagine it's tough to find five guys worth investing a ton of dough in. It's risky: How can he predict what the public is going to like?

It's also tough to find five guys who can mix together as a group and who will get along. Are their harmonies going to be cool? Is one guy going to be too difficult to go on the road with for three years? Are they really going to like each other in the end, or are they going to hate each other? So many little things come into play. I think it's tough work. It's really tough.

*There are a lot of people out there who just cannot sing, so when somebody could sing, he really got my attention.*

*– Jo Jo Wright*

Audioners had to show their moves as well as sing.

# The Hopefuls

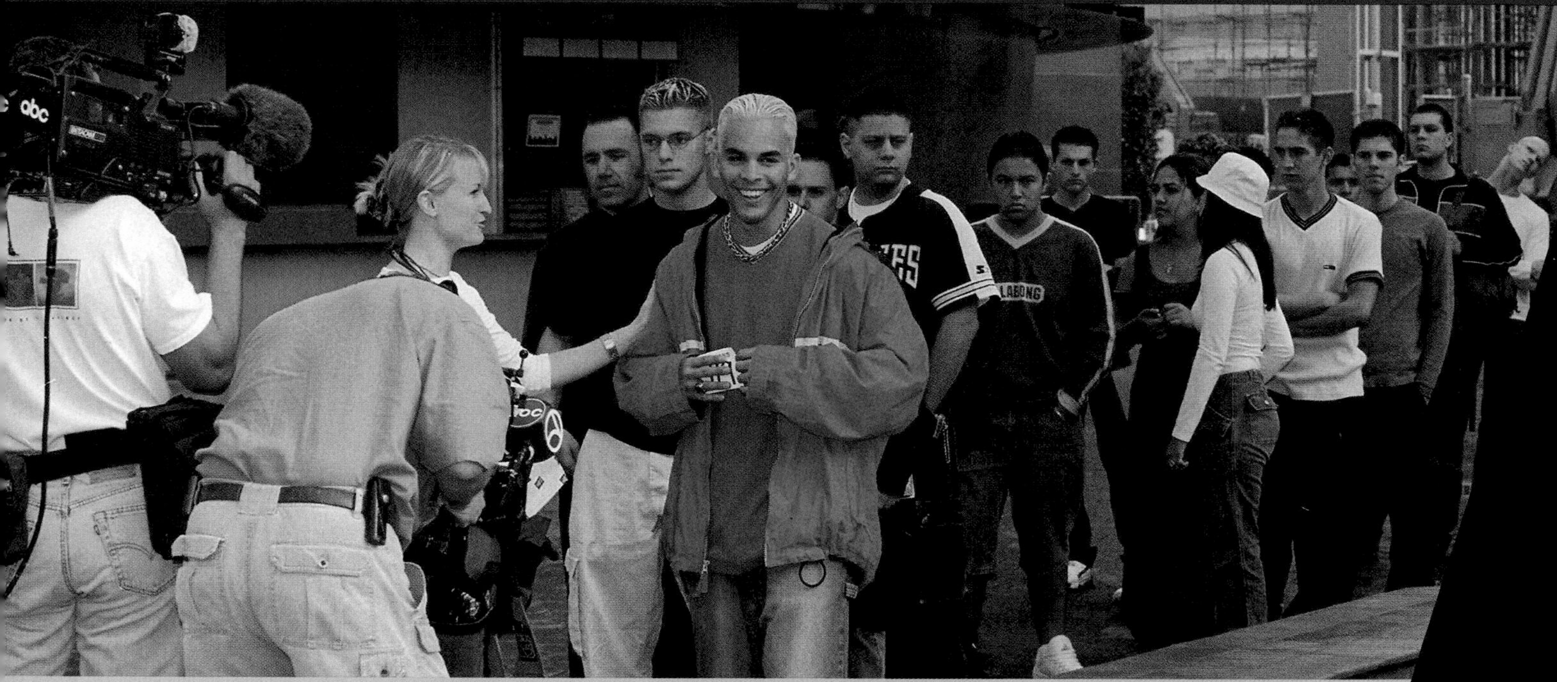

©2000 ABC, Inc / Scott Garfield

Pick me! Hundreds lined up to try out for O-TOWN.

25

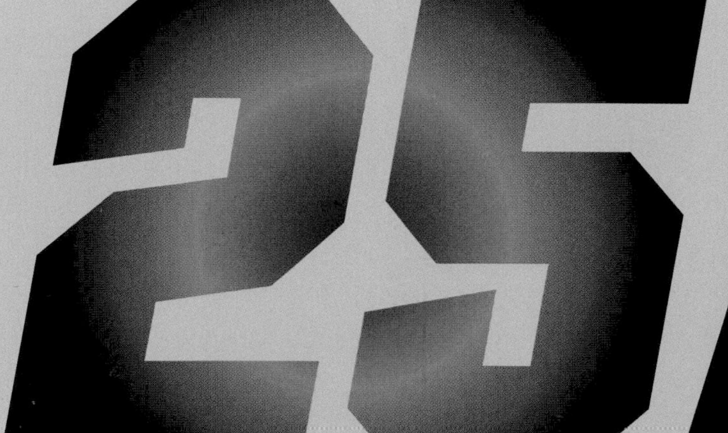

# Top 25

**THE EIGHT FINALISTS FROM THE TOP 25**

**Ashley Parker Angel**, 19, Redding, CA
**David Brooks**, 21, Jonesboro, AR
**Bryan Chan**, 26, Santa Barbara, CA
**Antonio Dennard**, 27, Orlando, FL
**Erik-Michael Estrada**, 21, Palm Bay, FL
**Christopher Gonzalez**, 22, Phoenix, AZ
**Roy Harcourt**, 21, New York, NY
**Ikaika Kahoano**, 22, Honolulu, HI
**Sam Lacy**, 20, Lewisville, TX
**Jesse Littleton**, 19, Sabina, OH
**Rik Mapes**, 24, Orlando, FL
**Paul Martin**, 22, Clinton, MS
**Mike Miller**, 20, Coral Springs, FL
**Steve Mooney**, 22, Orlando, FL
**Junior Mika**, 21, Honolulu, HI
**Dan Miller**, 20, Twinsburg, OH
**Clifton Oliver**, 24, Bronx, NY
**Trevor Penick**, 20, Rancho Cucamonga, CA
**Earl Robinson**, 19, Irving, TX
**Justin Roman**, 23, Bloomingdale, IL
**Jackie Salvucci**, 20, Medford, MA
**Jacob Underwood**, 20, El Cajon, CA
**Jason Waldrep**, 23, Honolulu, HI
**Jason Yeager**, 21, Grand Prairie, TX
**Matt Yoakum**, 20, Salem, OR

And then they were eight.

# The Eight Finalists

**Erik-Michael Estrada**

**Jacob Underwood**

**Trevor Penick**

**Mike Miller**

**Ashley Parker Angel**

**Paul Martin** (quit before the final cut)

**Bryan Chan**

**Ikaika Kahoano**

# The Final Five

5

***Ashley Parker Angel***

***Erik-Michael Estrada***

***Ikaika Kahoano*** *(quit; replaced by Dan Miller)*

***Trevor Penick***

***Jacob Underwood***

QUIT

Ikaika Kahoano

©2000 ABC, Inc / Bob d'Amico

replaced Ikaika

Jacob Underwood

Dan Miller

Erik-Michael Estrada

Ashley Parker Angel

Trevor Penick

Ben Van Hook

The eight finalists trying out for the final five cut.



## Brandon Sokun Taing,

**19, Silver Spring, Maryland**

My friend Amy walked up to me one day and said, "I just heard on MTV that Transcontinental Records is looking for a new boy band." Everybody always told me that I look and sound like a Backstreet Boy, so I thought, why not? I went down to Nashville and auditioned.

Honestly, I didn't know what I was doing. I sang the Backstreet Boys' "I Want It That Way" and 'N Sync's "Tearing Up My Heart." The singing was fine, but my dancing just killed it. I'm sort of like Ikaika. Sometimes I feel like my body wasn't made for dancing. That's why I didn't even make the top twenty-five.

I'd do it differently if I had to do it over again. I would have worked a lot harder on my dancing skills. I knew I could sing, but I just didn't think that dancing would be such a big part of it.

It was a really positive experience, though, because now I know what I really want to do with my life. After being on *Making the Band*, I made it into another group, called Unlimited. We're recording now, and things are going really well.

## Justin Roman,

**23, Bloomingdale, Illinois**

I had a pretty big dance single in Chicago called, "Push It Up," and I wanted to go national with my talent. O-Town seemed like the perfect opportunity.

I auditioned at the Hard Rock Cafe in Chicago. The *Chicago Sun-Times* ran a piece on me that came out that day. It was a full-page picture of me and the caption said: "*The next big thing*." They diagrammed my face, my body, and everything, pointing out what it takes to be in a boy band. That was before I even auditioned.

At the audition I busted out a rap that I wrote, then I sang "If I Ever Fall in Love." Then they asked me to sing a second song—"The Star Spangled Banner." I started it way too high, and when the high notes came, I couldn't hit them. I was so mad at myself! I cracked my voice and everything, so I was really disappointed. But the next thing I knew Lou Pearlman told me I was one of two finalists from Chicago, and he wanted me to come to Orlando. I was so excited I jumped up and gave Mr. Pearlman a hug.

Looking back on everything, I don't think I was even close to making the eight. My choreography scores were really high, but vocally, I know I wasn't strong enough.

Even though I didn't make it, my plan is still to be a huge star. Since *Making the Band* I compiled a demo CD. I'm shopping myself as a solo artist.

## Matt Yoakum,

**20, Salem, Oregon**

I went to the audition in Las Vegas because my friends wanted me to go. They picked three of us from there—me, Bryan Chan, and Ashley Angel—to go down to Orlando for the next cut. I had a disappointing time in Orlando because I hurt my back a couple of weeks earlier during track practice, so I couldn't dance. That pretty much knocked me out of contention.

If I had a chance to do it over again, I would definitely practice more, and I would have been more careful at track practice! I had a great time, though. I met a lot of people, and got a little glimpse of what the music industry is like.

Since then I got an internship at Disney World, so hopefully I can continue to pursue music in O-Town itself.

Even for the ones who didn't make the final five, it exposed them to show biz.

## Jackie Salvucci,

**20, Medford, Massachusetts**

Before the O-Town auditions, I was in a group and we were doing really well. We were going to get signed by the guy who put together New Kids on the Block. I even gave up a full scholarship for acting to be in that group. But it all fell through.

One day after that, I heard Carson Daly on *TRL* talk about the O-Town auditions, and I thought: *Here's my chance to be in a boy band.* There was a reason the first shot didn't work out, and this had to be it.

I went to the second day of auditions in New York. Four hundred kids showed up that day, and I was one of three they picked for the twenty-five. I was so excited I didn't sleep the night before I got on the plane to go to Orlando, and I didn't sleep the first night I got down there. It was overwhelming. My whole life I wanted to be a New Kid on the Block. I never had any professional dance or music training, but there I was in the top twenty-five in the country, and once again so close to being in a boy band.

When they picked the eight, and I wasn't one of them, I was very supportive to the guys who made it, but it was killing me inside. The guys that I bonded with most were all up on that stage. I wanted to be there too.

Overall, it was an incredible experience. It was the most positive experience I could have had even though it didn't work out the way I wanted it to. It made me fifty times stronger than I am because I always turn rejection into motivation.

# The Final Cut

**Lou Pearlman,** ***record executive:*** The final five represents the culmination of the judges' opinions, the feedback from the vocal and choreography coaches, and the production team's impressions of charisma and capability.

**Mark Goff,** ***vocal coach:*** A tough thing for me was deciding ultimately who was going to be chosen. What we see today was not what was on my list. As much as I think people would like to portray it as my decision, it wasn't. I contributed but I'm not sure that we were all looking for the same thing.

**Marc Piacenza,** ***road manager:*** I had a very good idea of who was going to be cut about two days before it was announced. To look at those two guys for those two days was awful. I became really emotional about it; it struck a chord in me because I was there from the get-go. In a very short time, I became emotionally tied to all these guys. There wasn't a dry eye in the house during the night of the cut.

**Tyjuan Jones,** ***choreographer:*** The hardest part of working with O-Town was watching the guys get cut from one phase to the next because I get attached to groups very quickly. I work with compassion, and it was difficult seeing twenty-five get cut down to eight, and eight get cut down to five.

Waiting around...the finalists before the cut.



*There wasn't a dry eye in the house during the night of the cut.*

*– Marc Piacenza*

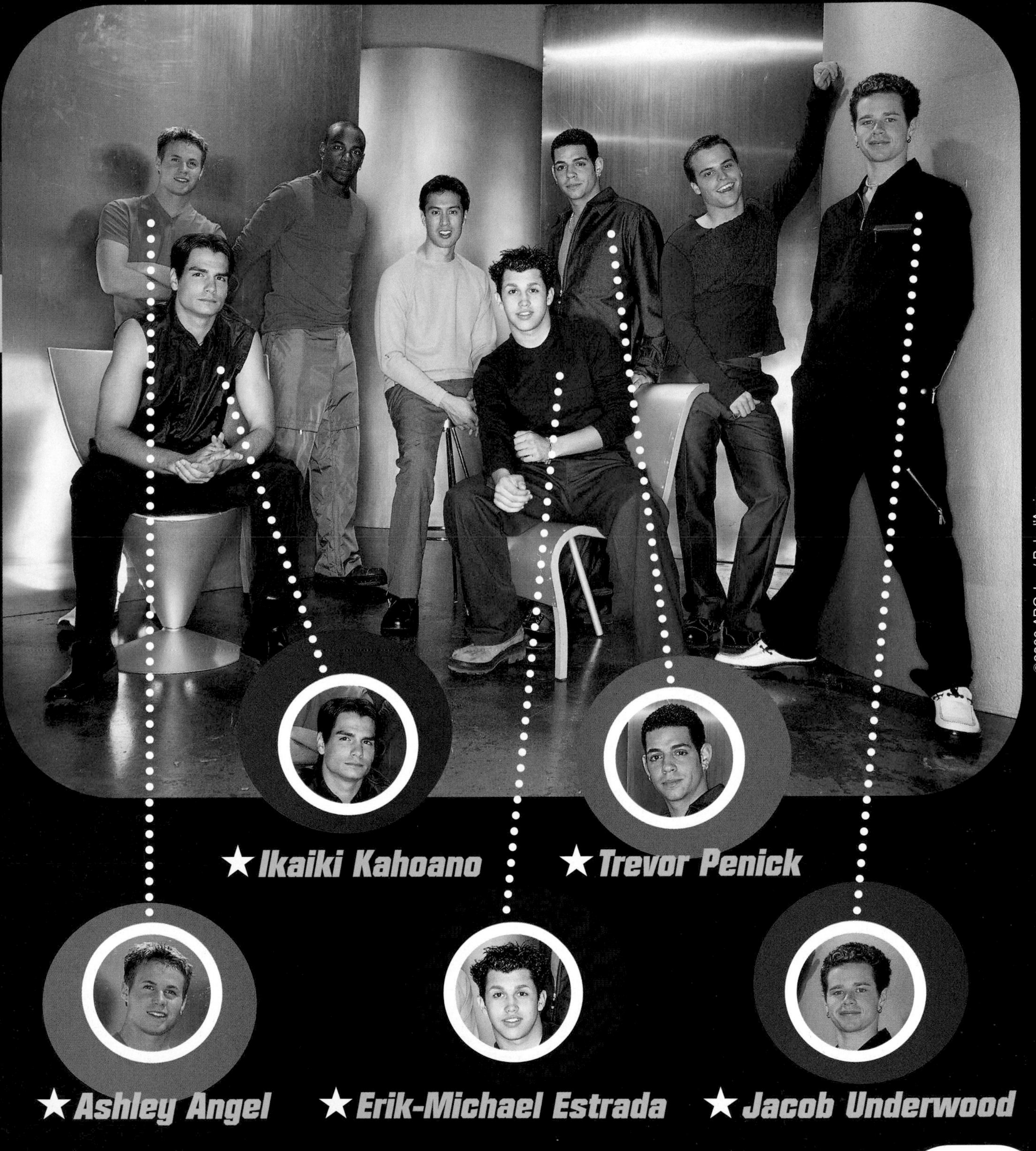

★Ashley Angel ★Erik-Michael Estrada ★Jacob Underwood

## Ashley Angel,

***19, Redding, California***

I didn't know quite how I would feel the night of the final cut. Because Paul left, two guys were going home instead of three, which made it a little harder, I think. The night that it happened, we were just pacing around the house for hours waiting for the contract. When it finally arrived, I just remember all of us being really pumped, and really excited. We signed it, then we sat down on the couch and we were all were holding hands. When Lou announced my name, I started to cry because it meant so much to me that I had actually made it.

I remember hugging Mike and Bryan and not wanting to let them go. I was so close to them. I knew that no matter which two didn't make it, it was going to hurt, but it was especially hard for me to say good-bye to Bryan because he was picked from the beginning with me in Vegas, and he was my roommate when we were twenty-five. It was hard with Mike, too, because Mike was my roommate at the house.

Mike and Bryan were the biggest men out of all of us that night, because they sucked up their emotions and were happy for us. They were like, "Let's take a picture with the five," and it felt weird because we had always posed for pictures as seven or as eight. They were standing behind the camera, and I didn't like it. I wanted them to be in front of the camera with the rest of us.

## Trevor Penick,

***21, Rancho Cucamonga, California***

It was a moment of triumph for me. My main goal in life was to become a performer, so it was a dream come true. I had just reached the highest goal that I ever set for myself. And to know that I was going to be doing what I love—that was very emotional.

## Erik-Michael Estrada,

***21, Palm Bay, Florida***

The night of the final cut was like an out-of-body experience. I had so much emotion going through my head. I was thinking about the guys, thinking about what I might have done to *not* get in—all before anything actually transpired. My brain was just going through so many different questions that I ended up kneeling down and praying for some peace.

I went in there knowing that I gave everything I had. I was dedicated and I loved the art, and if they saw that, then they were going to choose me. If they didn't feel what I had was good for the group, then they wouldn't have picked me, and I just would've had to live with that.

## Jacob Underwood,

***20, El Cajon, California***

It was weird because we signed the contract and it was a relief, and then there was excitement, and then the cut was happening. When it came down to the last name there were three guys sitting there and I thought, *God, right now, two guys are going to be so sad.*

Trevor, Jacob, Erik, Ashley

## Gone But Not Forgotten

# Michael Miller,

### 20, Coral Springs, Florida

No matter what names were called there were going to be certain levels of happiness for the guys who made it and sadness for the others, for not only losing a big opportunity but also a bunch of friends. Right when they started to call the names, my gut feeling kicked in, and I started thinking about what I was going to do next. It was really not as much of a shock as I expected it to be.

Trevor's reaction especially got to me. I was so happy for him because he was such a die-hard fan of every single pop artist out there, and now for him to be able to associate himself with them as colleagues was nice to see.

There was a definite difference between me and Bryan and the rest of the guys. The final five that were chosen looked great together and sounded good together. I think there would have been an odd one out if it was me or somebody else, and it wouldn't have been as good of a mix.

If I had to do it all over again I would try to become closer to the guys. I would be more concerned about maintaining camaraderie in the house as opposed to worrying about making the group.

I'll miss the comfort factor. It was comfortable being in a position where I could actually wake up in the morning, go to the rehearsal studio, and call that work. I'll miss living with all the guys, and the routine, knowing that we all were going to be doing the same thing everyday. I'll miss the entire atmosphere of O-Town, the whole experience, everything about it. I won't miss the cameras all that much, though.

*It was comfortable being in a position where I could actually wake up in the morning, go to the rehearsal studio, and call that work.*

The best part was realizing that I could still sing. Before the auditions, I had given up on it for a little while. Now I know I can actually make it in the industry. I was going to go back into modeling, but now I am going to go ahead and pursue music. Erik and I said when we first met, "Once you make it this far, there's no way you can turn back."

## Bryan Chan,

### 26, Santa Barbara, California

There was so much going through my head when the names were called for the final cut and I wasn't one of them. Disappointment, embarrassment, frustration, relief, but aside from what I was going through at that moment, I knew that five of my little brothers had realized a dream come true and I wanted to be there to support that and celebrate with them. I wanted to make the cut so badly, but in the end, when I had to go home, it was leaving my "new" family behind that hurt more than not making the final five. Because of the unique situation that we were in, we all became really close in a short amount of time, and going through so many new experiences together gave all of us a special relationship with one another.

We were all really talented in lots of different ways and we all had our strengths and our weaknesses, and I think any five of us could have made a great group. But any observer could see that most of the guys clicked together in a certain way, and I never felt like I was a part of that. There were two different mentalities in the house; we all loved music and wanted to make the final cut, but some of us applied more dedication and focus toward that common goal than others, yet some people let the cameras and all the added attention distract them.

I think I was probably too mature for O-Town. I don't mean to say that the others were immature, but I was the oldest and I had gone through so much in my life, which gave me a different take on things. My favorite times were just talking or hanging out with Ikaika and Mike. We seemed to share a common element of taking the experience as the chance of a lifetime and I think we treated it as such. I didn't want to go get tattoos with Erik and Jacob, or stay out till 4 am with the Herizon girls. In my eyes, I was there to prove that I had what it took to make the cut and that I was willing to earn it through my talent and dedication.

I can honestly say that there wasn't a single aspect of this project that I didn't have a good time doing. It's not just the dancing, the studio work, or the cameras buzzing. The eight of us were a very diverse crowd and I ended up learning something from each of them. Everything had its purpose and gave me something to take away from the experience, from the personal interviews that made me ask some pretty introspective questions, to the disagreements we had within the group–it all taught me something about myself.

The experience really taught me that a lifelong dream could come true if you want it bad enough, work hard and create your own opportunities. I had wanted to sing all my life, but I never pushed myself to take the leap, it took going through this process to realize how much I really want it and how bad I'm willing to work for it. If I had given up after the first time someone said I wasn't good enough or that I didn't have the right look, or they didn't think I'd be able to handle it, I would never have gone to the O-Town audition.

Bryan Chan



*I think that I was probably too mature for O-Town.*

# Dropouts

## Paul Martin, 22, Clinton, Mississippi

Over Christmas break I decided that being a part of O-Town wasn't the right opportunity for me, so when I came back, I quit. I left because, honestly, I just wasn't happy with the way the group was going. So, I think for their sake, and for my sake, I had to back out.

I loved all the guys, actually. I got along with all of them great, and I miss them to death. But I felt the unnecessary drama was hindering the music, and I couldn't deal with the lack of personal space with the cameras around. You don't realize how much you value your personal time until you don't have it anymore. I think that was the toughest part for me.

It was a hard decision to leave, but I'm glad I did it. All the guys were really supportive. Actually, Trevor was angry with me, because we were pretty tight. But it all worked out well, and we're all still friends.

Right after the episode where I leave aired, a woman came up to me at church and hit me! She slapped me on the shoulder, and asked: "Why did you leave?" That was probably the weirdest experience I've ever had.

I look at being in O-Town as one of the pinnacle experiences of my life. I've grown so much from it, and so much happened in that short amount of time. I'm gaining a lot from it. It's been completely positive, careerwise.

I learned a lot from the whole experience. I learned what I really wanted. I learned how to deal with people. I learned that the business itself is tough, but I also learned that it's the business I want to be in.

I'm much happier now. I'm singing in a group in Nashville called Marshal Dyllon, and we're working with Kenny Rogers, so it's really cool. Country music has always been a big part of my life.

If I had to do it all over again, I wouldn't be as big a flirt! It all came across different than it actually was. I think they got an accurate aspect of only one part of my personality. There's a lot more to me.

Paul Martin



*It was a hard decision to leave, but I'm glad I did it.*

Ikaika with the guys before he quit.

# On Paul

***Jacob:*** We were completely shocked when Paul quit. Completely shocked.

***Ashley:*** I never had expected Paul, out of everyone, to leave. So when he left it really confused me. I really liked him and I really thought he was going to make it to the five. But, I just realized that something in his heart told him he wasn't supposed to be there. I knew it had to be a pretty big reason for him to leave this kind of opportunity. The good thing is he did it at a time where it really didn't affect the rest of us too badly.

***Erik:*** When Paul quit, I figured there was a story behind it that we didn't know. I'm glad he left when he did, before the final five were picked.

***Trevor:*** I was very surprised, and I was very sad, because I had gotten really close to Paul. I still really don't know why he did it.

***Lou Pearlman, record executive:*** I don't think Paul wanted to see the rejection if there was going to be one, and I don't think this is the style of music he really wanted. He's more into a country mix, and now I think that he has found that.

Circular photos: ©2000 ABC, Inc / Bob d'Amico; Lou Pearlman by Lorenzo Bevilaqua

## Ikaika Kahoano,

***22, Honolulu, Hawaii***

*(Ikaika opted not to participate in this book project. All quotes are taken from his on-camera interviews with* Making the Band's *producers and directors.)*

[Being in O-Town] wasn't my dream. It totally wasn't. I didn't think singing and dancing would be this hard. It's a hell of a lot of pressure.

It's the hardest thing I've ever had to do. I don't want to let people down. I just want to be myself. But it's hard to be yourself in a business . . . that doesn't care about you.

# On Ikaika



**Jay Marose, publicist:** Ikaika showed up one day with his brother and announced that he was quitting. We had to shoot commercials for the show that day, so we asked Ikaika if he would at least stay the day. Ikaika said yes, but his brother said no. We ended up hiring a stand-in for the commercials.

**Ashley:** I respect that Ikaika left because that's what he wanted to do in his heart, but I was upset at first. I really liked Ikaika and I felt like I was close with him. But he quit right in the middle of a big photo shoot, and he didn't finish it because his brother said he couldn't. This upset me, that he wouldn't at least tell his brother he was going to finish this photo shoot with us. I felt like he owed us that. Now that I know he would have actually quit sooner if his family had let him, I'm not as upset. But I do respect that he didn't let it go on for another six months, have us be on tour somewhere, and then say, "Guys, I'm going home." There's no prime time to have that happen, but at least he did it when we could still pick up the pieces and get another guy. So I can't continue to be mad at him. It all worked out for the best. And he's doing what makes him happy now, so I'm glad for him.

**Erik:** When Ikaika left, it seemed like it was supposed to happen. But he surprised us, in a way. We thought it was finally working out. He surprised us because of the timing, but I guess it really wasn't a big surprise he made that decision.

**Jacob:** I didn't say "I told you so" or anything. I believe whatever happens is meant to happen, and I knew it happened for a reason. I was completely annoyed with it, but I'm over it.

**Trevor:** It wasn't much of a shock. He was always missing home and his girlfriend. We were frustrated, though, because none of us thought he should have made the group in the first place. He said: "If I make this group, guys, I'm not going to quit. I'm going to be 110 percent into it." Then he makes it, and then a month later, he quits! There are no hard feelings, though. I like Ikaika a lot.

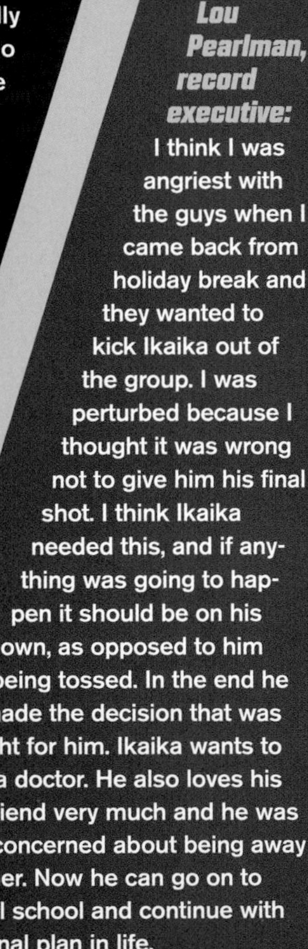

**Lou Pearlman, record executive:** I think I was angriest with the guys when I came back from holiday break and they wanted to kick Ikaika out of the group. I was perturbed because I thought it was wrong not to give him his final shot. I think Ikaika needed this, and if anything was going to happen it should be on his own, as opposed to him being tossed. In the end he made the decision that was right for him. Ikaika wants to be a doctor. He also loves his girlfriend very much and he was very concerned about being away from her. Now he can go on to medical school and continue with his original plan in life.

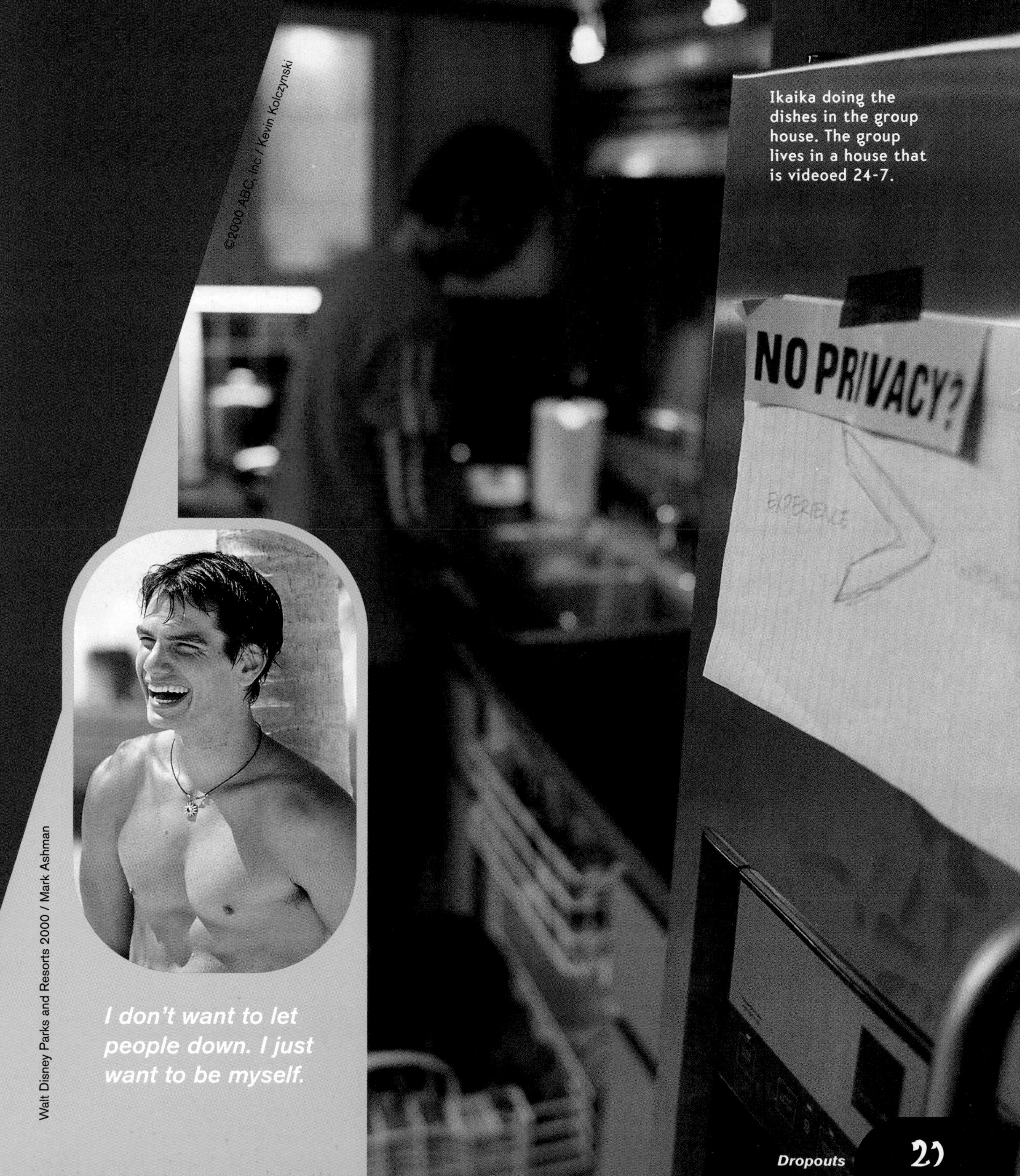


Ikaika doing the dishes in the group house. The group lives in a house that is videoed 24-7.





*I don't want to let people down. I just want to be myself.*

# The Fifth Element

## Jay Marose, *publicist*

Shortly after Ikaika quit, I was at the movies with the guys, and I went to the concession stand with Jacob and Erik. While there I asked, "Who do you think the fifth member should be?" They said they had never talked about it, but they each had some idea. I said, "Why don't you both whisper who you think into each of my ears." They both whispered "Dan Miller," who was from the top twenty-five. When we walked into the theater, I asked the same question to Ashley and Trevor. They also said "Dan Miller."

The next morning we found out that Lou had been auditioning people at his house. The guys weren't happy about this, because they really wanted to talk to him about Dan. So, they went over there and told him they wanted Dan to be the fifth member, and Lou said, "Get him down here."

I was incredibly supportive of that move because Dan had made such an impression on me at the Nashville auditions. He walked in and he made the entire experience better for everybody there, including us. He had so much personality and he was so upbeat, and he rolled with everything we threw at him. He's just really genuine, and really animated.

I was so moved because I think so highly of Dan as a person, and these guys, who had been kind of irresponsible, really took charge for once. When Dan arrived, they gave him a warm welcome and treated him like an equal from the first day.

## Dan Miller

After the cut from the twenty-five, I went back to school and resumed my life. One night I was studying for an exam and I got a phone call from Lou Pearlman. He said, "I'm here with the O-Town guys," and I thought I was getting a call from them to check up on me and to see what I was doing, because there was a lot of talk about reuniting and staying friends from the twenty-five.

Then Lou started to explain what happened with Ikaika, and then he asked if I was willing to come down to Orlando to be in the group! I couldn't believe it—I didn't know what to say. I called my parents and my close friends right afterward, and the next morning I was on a flight to Orlando.

I never took that exam! I left during the busiest week I had all year in school. I had three exams that week and two big projects due. And I just let it all go. I thought if it doesn't work, then I'll come back, take the exams, and suffer all the consequences. But I had to take the opportunity while it was there.

The guys told me about the night they were all at the movie theater with our publicist, Jay, and how they all told him separately they wanted me as the fifth member. I was severely lucky. I mean, I wasn't in touch with these guys or anything. I guess I made a good enough impression in Orlando during the top twenty-five that they wanted me back.



*I was severely lucky.*

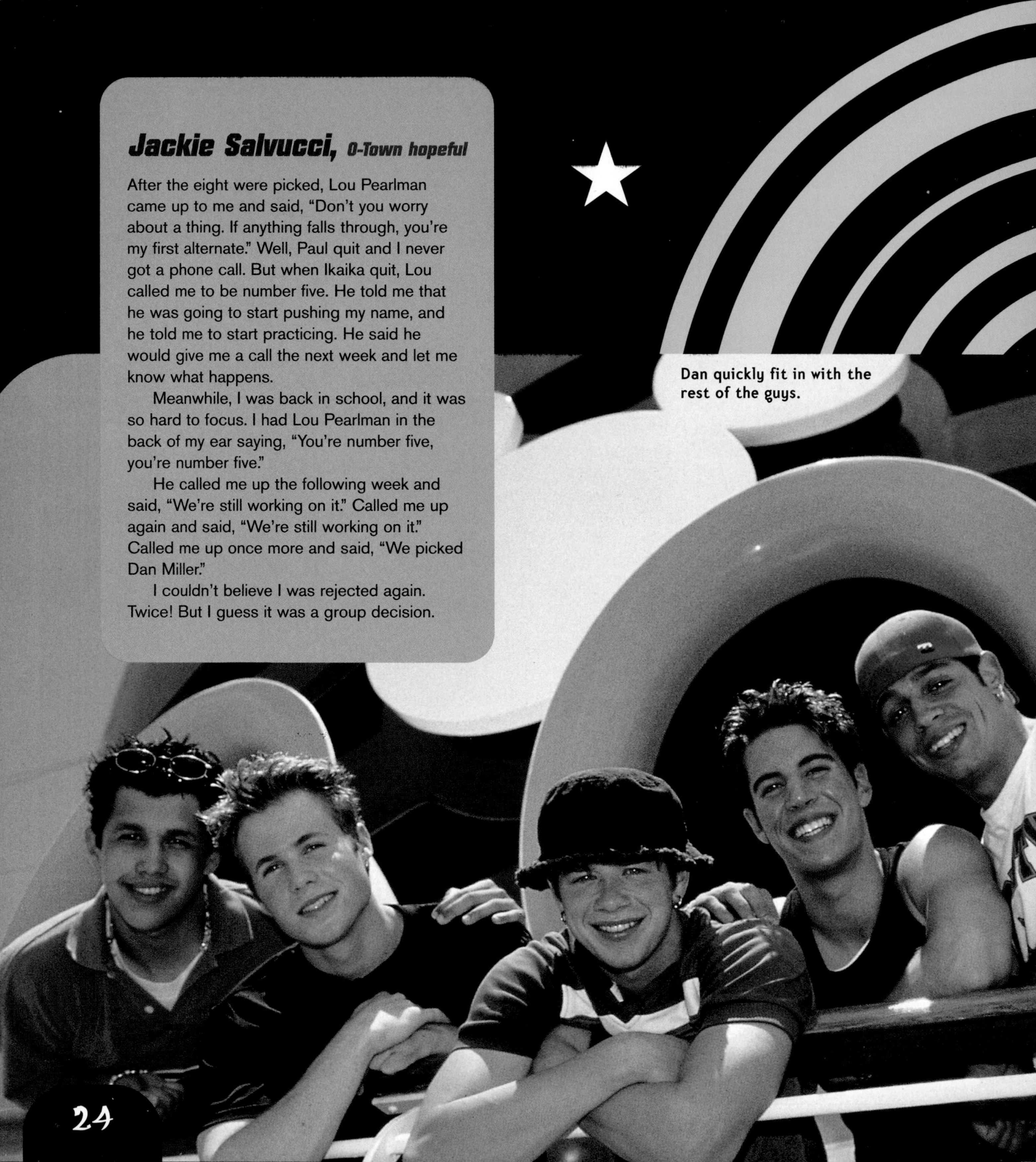

## ***Jackie Salvucci,*** *O-Town hopeful*

After the eight were picked, Lou Pearlman came up to me and said, "Don't you worry about a thing. If anything falls through, you're my first alternate." Well, Paul quit and I never got a phone call. But when Ikaika quit, Lou called me to be number five. He told me that he was going to start pushing my name, and he told me to start practicing. He said he would give me a call the next week and let me know what happens.

Meanwhile, I was back in school, and it was so hard to focus. I had Lou Pearlman in the back of my ear saying, "You're number five, you're number five."

He called me up the following week and said, "We're still working on it." Called me up again and said, "We're still working on it." Called me up once more and said, "We picked Dan Miller."

I couldn't believe I was rejected again. Twice! But I guess it was a group decision.

Dan quickly fit in with the rest of the guys.

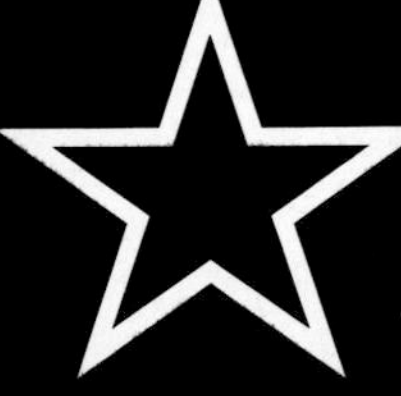

## Lou Pearlman, *record executive*

©2000 ABC, Inc / Lorenzo Bevilaqua

It was a group decision. When Ikaika left we had to replace him with another person who would be a tenor. Mike Miller, for example, wasn't a tenor, so vocally we had to find someone to fit the bill. The guys wanted Dan Miller, who I remembered from the top twenty-five as a really great dancer. We needed somebody who could move. Ikaika didn't have that capability, so we thought Dan would add some flavor to the mix.

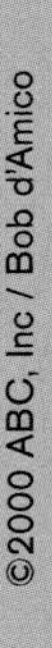

Walt Disney Parks and Resorts 2000

## Ashley Angel

©2000 ABC, Inc / Bob d'Amico

The motivational speaker Tony Robbins came and spent a day with us after Ikaika quit. At the time we thought we were going to stay as a four-member group, but he was instrumental in persuading us to be five. He talked about the power of five, the strength of five as a number, and vocally, five guys sound better than four do. So we decided we wanted another member.

We didn't know what to do at first, if we should pick a brand-new guy, pick someone from the twenty-five, or what. When we decided to pick from the twenty-five, we all decided on Dan.

It was so strange because we had never talked about it, but we unanimously picked him. He came right away, and he fit in perfectly. He picked up the dance steps immediately and he got his vocal parts down quickly. I have no idea why Dan didn't make it to the eight in the first place. But I'm awfully glad he's with us now.

# Boy Band Boot Camp

## Singing 101

### Mark Goff, *vocal coach*

I had worked with groups like the Backstreet Boys, 'N Sync, and C Note in the past, but working with O-Town was a completely different experience. It took quite a long time for the guys to understand the parameters involved, and it definitely made my job more difficult. Plus, they were getting the red carpet treatment before they paid any dues, so it was really hard at first to get them to focus.

We would spend two to six hours together at a time. I think consistency is important in education, so we always got started the same way. We'd begin with breathing exercises and warm-ups, and then we'd move on to part-singing. But it didn't always go the way I planned. There were a lot of distractions—the cameras, the record company people coming in, Lou and all of his people. None of it helped the guys focus.

When the cameras went away it was a huge relief for me. I think the kids were able to relax and be themselves more. I hate to admit it, but every time the cameras were around the guys were just on, and I was just trying to do my gig and I wasn't sure if I was reaching the individual. When the cameras went away, all the glamour went away. All of a sudden it started becoming a much more real situation.

There was a point when I had to consider whether I should stay involved in the project or not, because the guys weren't getting it. They weren't bringing their tapes to rehearsals, and it was evident they weren't rehearsing outside of my instruction. I felt like I was becoming ineffective because they weren't stepping up to the plate.

Part of what encouraged me to stay were my ethics of being a teacher. I could see the kids weren't getting it, and I was frustrated that, as a teacher, I hadn't helped them. But I have a "never give up" attitude. If I don't teach them, who's going to?

The best part was seeing the growth of each of those guys individually, watching them come into their own as young men and finally understand what it is they're really involved in. It took a long time for us to get there, but they are much stronger and better-grounded individuals now.

# Dancing 101

## Raymond Del Barrio, *choreographer*

We would start out every day by getting the guys physically warm first, and then we'd go into choreography. We would try to do as much as we possibly could in the short amount of time we had—I tried my best to cram in all the information I could—and a lot of times the boys were late.

I don't think we spent enough time on the development. Roughly three hours a day, for me, is not enough to get the quality Lou was after. Lou wanted the Rolls-Royce of boys groups and I told him that could happen, but it would have to be very intense.

If there were no cameras, I think I would have been a lot harder on them. I would have been able to really tear them apart. But I suppose the cameras did keep me from doing that, which for their sake was probably good. But Tyjuan, Mark, and I still did a good job of letting them know what they were and weren't doing well.

Learning how to bust some moves.



## Tyjuan Jones, *choreographer*

Most people don't understand the endurance your body has to have to get on stage night after night and sing and dance at the same time. We did—and continue to do—a lot of physical training in addition to dancing. I still make them jog around the building and sing at the same time. And we still do crunches, push-ups, and go to the gym after every rehearsal.

# Discipline

## Marc Piacenza, *road manager*

I hope I've taught the guys how to become more responsible and appreciate the gift that has been given to them by MTV and Transcontinental—this is a once-in-a-lifetime opportunity. Although the boys are very well grounded, I just kept trying to reiterate throughout our time together how important it was to be a good role model and to set a good example.

They had a different setup than any other music group I had worked with before. There were the cameras, of course, and the house. Other up-and-coming bands don't get a house on a lake with its own private beach and cameras following them everywhere plus catered food and a free car! I think the whole show changed the dynamic of what it takes to achieve success as a pop group.

The angriest I ever became with the guys was at the New Year's Eve party, when they acted up and drew unnecessary attention to themselves. I was just ballistic! It's true that boys will be boys, and yes, they still have a lot to learn, but they were begged: "Please don't stand out in this crowd." Guys from Backstreet were in the crowd, record producers, Lou Pearlman himself. They had to act accordingly, and they didn't.

It's not that they dropped the ball, it's just that they forgot where they were. I take some of the blame for that too. I was letting them be. This was our night to have fun, but I should have been there to police them a little more.

The Georgia show was when I was most proud of them. They got out there and just nailed it. They really, really, really worked to get to that level. What takes most bands a year, they had to learn in two months. So it was just amazing how everything came together.

Erik kicking back after a long day of practice.

# The Trainees

**Ashley:** It's definitely boot camp, but a good boot camp. Nobody realizes how much work is involved to get something like this up and running. There was a lot of pressure on us, but when you spend every single day in rehearsal, your singing and dancing has to get better. I've grown as a performer, but I still want to get even better. There's no end point for me.

**Jacob:** It's a lot harder than I expected, and we make it hard on ourselves. We pride ourselves on being perfectionists, so we're constantly working.

We were famous before we were good, and we've had to take a lot of big steps along the way. That takes a lot of work, but I've always worked hard when it comes to music. Music to me was always this intense.

**Erik:** A lot of people think we just get up and sing and dance, but it's not that simple. It's a lot of training and a lot of discipline and focus. You have to want it more than anything, because it requires your all. It requires your mind, body, and soul.

The intense training humbled me and strengthened my ability to work within a group. Before, as an only child, I never had to share anything. Plus, I had to break myself down to a certain extent so I could actually hear criticism and appreciate where it's coming from. Constructive criticism only makes you better. You weigh it out, and you see if it's solid, and you apply it and see how it works, and if it doesn't then you try something else. I credit Mark Goff with making me ten times a better singer than I was two months ago.

I think right now the most trying thing about training is going to the gym even if I want to go home and go to sleep after six hours of dancing and singing. That's probably the most difficult part for me.

**Dan:** I didn't know it was going to be this much work, but I love it. There's so many people out there who want to be singers and don't get to do it everyday like I do. It's the hardest and easiest job in the world because I'm doing something I love.

I'm a hard worker, and I like working. When I came in the first day and I was told that I had dance rehearsal for eight hours the next day, I couldn't wait. I was just ready to work and ready to handle business.

Our coaches are very hard on us because they want us to be good. It stinks when you're getting yelled at, but later, you appreciate it. We know that we have lots of potential, and these people are just trying to help us.

**Trevor:** Dancing is the most grueling part for me because it makes me sweat the most for the longest amount of time. We dance for four or five hours straight sometimes, and then go to the gym right after that.

No one likes to take criticism but once you learn to take it in and do what needs to be done to fix something . . . when you see the results it's so worth it. I felt that it all paid off especially during our Georgia show. It was there we all finally clicked and all our hard work showed. We had rehearsed so much that when we did it, it all came together very well.

Circular photos: ©2000 ABC, Inc / Bob d'Amico; except Dan Miller photo by Walt Disney Parks and Resorts 2000 / Mark Ashman

# Hit or Miss: Will O-Town Make It?

## Mark Goff, vocal coach

Ultimately, it's the public who will decide if they are going to take the money out of their pockets and buy O-Town's record or not. Whether they end up being the best singing group in the world or not remains to be seen. I spent two and a half years developing the Backstreet Boys, and it was two years before they even got a record deal. So O-Town's schedule was really accelerated.

I don't think their heads were in the game for the right reasons in the beginning, but eventually that changed. At first, they just wanted to be famous. I told them, "If you are fame-driven, eventually you're going to fall. If you base how you approach what you do on being good at what you do, you'll get what's coming to you."

## Jo Jo Wright, DJ, KISS FM, Los Angeles

They have a real good chance, being on TV and having people getting to know them. So it's not like they are totally new when they put on a concert or when the CD hits the stores.

I'll be glad to see them finally make it after all they went through. Everything else up to this points to something good happening. But it can end real quickly.

### *Tyjuan Jones,* choreographer

I think they have no choice! We're going to see to it that they *do* make it. As long as they look to the people who are looking out for their best interests, then they definitely have no choice but to be successful.

### *Raymond Del Barrio,* choreographer

There's no reason why they shouldn't make it, but quite frankly, like I say in the show: they ain't got nothing on 'N Sync and the Backstreet Boys. 'N Sync and Backstreet Boys worked for years. O-Town had every chance that the opportunity can afford them. They'd better be damn good.

Walt Disney Parks and Resorts 2000 / Mark Ashman

# Part Two

# O-TOWN

Ben Van Hook

# The Final Five

Ben Van Hook

# Trevor Penick

## Fast Facts

**Birthdate:** November 16, 1979

**Sign:** Scorpio

**Hometown:** Rancho Cucamonga, CA

**Family:** mom, Doris; dad, Clifton; sisters Traci, thirty-one; Rani, twenty-four; and Vanessa, fifteen.

**Favorite band:** Boyz II Men.

**Favorite book:** Catcher in the Rye by J. D. Salinger

**Favorite TV show:** Saved by the Bell

**Favorite movie:** Billy Madison

**Favorite actor:** Denzel Washington

**Favorite actress:** Jennifer Love Hewitt

**Favorite thing to do when he's not working:** relaxing

**Favorite food:** cereal

**What's in his Walkman:** Maxwell: Unplugged

**Professional role model:** Will Smith

I was "Mr. Trash" before I joined O-Town. While attending Cal State Fullerton, I worked at a minor-league baseball stadium picking up trash and entertaining fans, and that was my nickname—Mr. Trash. I'd dress up in a tuxedo, walk around the stadium, and pick up garbage, but I'd also entertain the fans in between innings by dancing on the field with the mascot. Sometimes four of my buddies and I would do a Backstreet Boys routine on the dugout.

I miss being "Mr. Trash" because it was such a fun job. I loved the fans, and the best part was being able to make little kids smile all the time. But I know I'm going to be making a lot of people smile now, too.

All my life I've been trying to make people smile. When I played shortstop on a baseball team I would

**Kicking it tropical style. Trevor with Jacob and Ashley.**

literally perform on the field, doing things on the sidelines to make people laugh.

In seventh grade I took my first acting class. That's when I knew for sure that I wanted to do something with entertainment. From there I moved on to school plays, a short film for my high school, and majoring in theater in college. But I never formally studied music or dancing.

Dancing somehow came naturally to me. I guess I was just born with a lot of rhythm. As far as singing goes, I'm still learning. Everyone grows up singing in the shower, singing their favorite songs all the time, but every time I would sing, people would beg me to shut up! I didn't know how to use my voice back then.

I was really lucky that I made it into O-Town so I could actually get training to learn how to sing. Working with the vocal coach made me a hundred times more of a singer than I was before. I actually consider myself a singer now.

## Making the Cut

My best friend was the one who found out about the O-Town auditions. He works for the school paper at our college and he's always on the Internet. He found an announcement that Lou Pearlman was doing a nationwide talent search for the next boy band, and he knew that was just right up my alley. We were big fans of the Backstreet Boys at the time, and we even waited in a big, long line with ten thousand screaming teenagers for tickets to the *Millennium* show. So when we saw the announcement we were like: *This is so us!*

The deadline to send a tape was in three days. So we made a tape that day and sent it out. Then we went to the audition. And here I am.

I think I was picked to be in O-Town because it shows that I love to entertain. I think I have a lot of heart and a good stage presence, and the judges noticed that. If I didn't make it, I'd be back at Cal State, pursuing theater. One way or another I'd make it in this business!

## *Living in a Fishbowl*

Generally, I'm happier without the cameras around, but other times, I think: *God, I wish the cameras were here to see this.* Like when we do something really, really *good.* I always wish at those moments that the cameras were there. But then when we do something bad, I'm relieved. I'm like, *thank the Lord the cameras aren't here!* In the beginning, the first two weeks, I was constantly thinking about what I was doing, but after that, I don't think it mattered to anyone at all. I forgot the cameras were there.

It was hard having no privacy. There were times when I just wanted to sit in my room and think about home, and the cameras would be right there, watching me think. But I think the whole thing with the cameras was that they wanted us to be ourselves–they wanted the audience to see us being ourselves.

It's hard to watch the show now because in the beginning we sucked! It was hard for eight different people to be mixed and matched and have a good sound together. Whenever they show that, I'm like, *oh God, no.* But after they picked the five, and we started to progress, I found it easier to take.

Ben Van Hook

***All my life I've been trying to make people smile.***

# Trevor's Mom,
## Doris

When the show first came on TV, our phone was ringing off the hook! People we hadn't spoken to in years were calling because they had seen Trevor on TV.

Trevor was always entertaining our family. The first time I noticed his talent was when he was eight or nine years old. He'd always entertain everybody with his dancing at New Year's Eve parties, or weddings, but it only occurred to me for the first time last year, at a family reunion when he took over the dance floor by himself, that he might become a performer someday.

Last year at my daughter's thirtieth birthday party, everyone dressed up like people from the Eighties, and Trevor dressed like Michael Jackson. He and a friend did a whole dance routine to "Beat It," and he knew every move, every facial expression that Michael Jackson did in the video. We have it on tape and it's really funny to watch.

The Trevor I know is sweet, energetic, and always on the move. He likes to make things happen, like his father. Wherever he went, he liked to be the center of attention. He could always make me laugh.

I wish Trevor big success. I do worry about him getting taken advantage of in the music business because he trusts a lot of people, which is good and bad.

It's hard to have Trevor three thousand miles away. It's frustrating not to be able to hop in the car and drive to see him like when he was at school. He does come home and surprise us once in a while. But I miss talking to him as much as I'm used to.

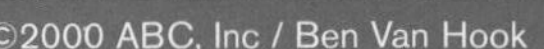

## Fame

I don't really know if I want to be a star. What I do know is that I want to entertain. I just want to make people happy. I love to see little kids' faces when they see me and know who I am. When I sign autographs for them it's great to see them just light up. To know that I can make someone's day–that's a great thing.

I think it's great if I'm just walking down the street and someone I've never seen before says, "Hey, Trevor!" That's the thing about our show–people feel as if they know us on a personal level. It's not just like they see us on stage, and see us in magazines and read about us. The show has a personal touch.

The most thrilling moment has to be seeing fans go wild during a show. That really pumps me up. There's no way I can get tired onstage with people screaming for me. It's what I've worked my whole life for, and when it's actually happening, I'm the happiest person alive.

I absolutely love what I'm doing. But sometimes I miss the simple things, like walking through the halls at school. Sometimes, certain smells come to me and remind me of things that I miss. I'll smell something and think, *that smells like the theater building at school.*

Remembering those things helps me keep my feet on the ground. That and just staying myself is all I can do. I don't think I've changed much through this whole experience. I'm still Trevor.

Homesick Trevor often thinks of his friends and family when he's on the road.

Ben Van Hook

Trevor met bandmate Jacob at the first day of auditions in L.A. The pair have been tight ever since.

*The most thrilling moment has to be seeing fans go wild during a show. That really pumps me up.*

## Family

It was so hard to leave my family behind, and to do it so quickly. It's hard to know I won't see them consistently for a very long time, but they were all so supportive. I just had so much love at home, and getting pulled out of my life like that was tough. I miss my family all the time, but I never, ever think about quitting.

When I first started this I was worried about my little sister, Vanessa, the most, just because she's in high school and I don't want people to either hate her or like her because of me. But she's doing really well, much to my relief.

## Girls, Girls, Girls

It's kind of easy to meet a lot of girls now but I don't ever try to bring up the show or the band when I meet anyone. I don't like to talk about it, and I don't want someone to like me just because I'm in a band. I actually don't have a lot of time to meet people right now.

When I do date someone she has to have a sense of humor, and I like someone who's a dancer. Not a professional dancer, but someone who loves to dance and can go all night. I also would like to meet someone who comes from a good family, who's into having a good family. And a good heart is essential.

Walt Disney Parks and Resorts 2000 / Mark Ashman

Trevor had a blast on the dance floor of Orlando's retro disco 8 Trax.

Trevor Penick

## Is There Life After O-Town?

Definitely. If we are not together in ten or fifteen years I see myself doing film.

Ben Van Hook

# On Trevor

**Ashley:** My first impression of Trevor was that he was nervous, but I didn't know why. When we were twenty-five, I remember he came up and said, "Man, you have some vocals, boy!" And I said, "So do you! You're going to do really well." And he was like, "No, no, I don't know, I don't know." And I had seen him dance, and I didn't see why he should be so nervous, because he has everything.

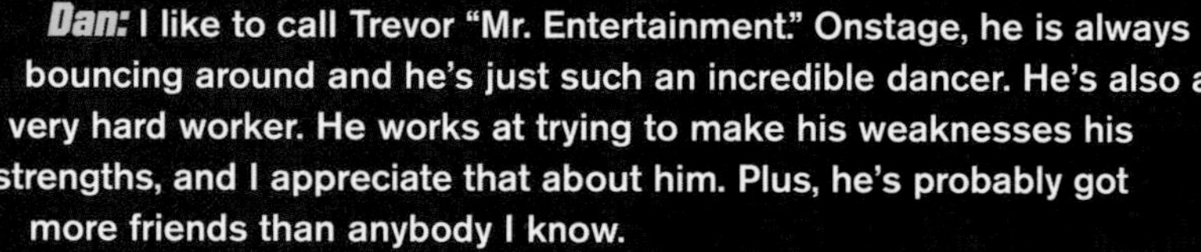

**Dan:** I like to call Trevor "Mr. Entertainment." Onstage, he is always bouncing around and he's just such an incredible dancer. He's also a very hard worker. He works at trying to make his weaknesses his strengths, and I appreciate that about him. Plus, he's probably got more friends than anybody I know.

**Erik:** Trevor is the emotional heart of this group. He wants it so bad, and he wants to be better, and yearns to be better. Whenever I need a reality check of how much I want to be a part of this, I just go to him. That's one of the reasons why I chose to live with him, because I know how dedicated he is. And I want to be as close to that as possible; it's always good to have someone like him around to refocus you.

**Jacob:** I have a really close bond to Trevor because we're the only two to follow each other the whole way in this process. I met him at the very first audition in L.A. He's one of the closest friends I've ever had. He's fun to be around—he's the life of the party, and never loses his energy.

**Mark Goff, vocal coach:** Trevor has made great improvements, particularly in his part-singing. His willingness to work and accept criticism and apply it is helping him get the job done. And that's really what it's about.

**Marc Piacenza, road manager:** Trevor is down-to-earth, appreciates everything, and has worked his butt off to get to where he is. And he's probably the best dancer I've ever seen.

**Tyjuan Jones, choreographer:** Trevor is definitely the most highly energetic person I've ever met. His dancing is great, and he's definitely a well-rounded entertainer.

**Raymond Del Barrio, choreographer:** Trevor works so hard. He worked his butt off, and he knows that he made O-Town because of it.

**Trevor on Trevor:** I think I bring energy to the group, a performance level that everyone can match up to.

Circular photos: ©2000 ABC, Inc / Bob d'Amico; except Dan Miller photo by Walt Disney Parks and Resorts 2000 / Mark Ashman

*I like to call Trevor 'Mr. Entertainment.' Onstage, he is always bouncing around and he's just such an incredible dancer.*

*— Dan Miller*

Walt Disney Parks and Resorts 2000 / Mark Ashman

# ERIK

Ben Van Hook

Walt Disney Parks and Resorts 2000 / Mark Ashman

# Erik-Michael Estrada

## Fast Facts

**Birthdate:** September 23, 1979

**Sign:** Libra

**Hometown:** Palm Bay, FL

**Family:** mom, Micki; dad, Mel

**Favorite band:** Can't pick just one!

**Favorite book:** Animal Farm by George Orwell

**Favorite TV show:** The Simpsons

**Favorite movie:** Happy Gilmore

**Favorite actor:** Al Pacino

**Favorite actress:** Michelle Pfeiffer

**Favorite thing to do when he's not working:** driving

**Favorite food:** sushi

**What's in his Walkman:** Steve Miller Band

**Professional role model:** Aerosmith

I was traumatized onstage when I was pretty young, so it's amazing that I ever got back on. I was singing at a performance that marked the closing down of my elementary school. I was in that school since kindergarten, so they asked me and four others who had been there from the beginning to sing and dance. During the song, I looked at the front row where the faculty was sitting. My mom was there, too, because she was part of the faculty. They were all crying, and I just lost it, and started crying on stage. My friend next to me had to take my part.

After that, it was really hard for me to get onstage, because I had lost my poise. That is a big no-no. You can't lose your poise onstage—that is a time when you have to be able to have total control.

After that, I had a calling inside me, an unfulfilling feeling every time I would see people onstage. Slowly, I worked my way back on.

First, it was just getting together with school buddies and singing. And then, senior year of high school, I started to excel at classical music. I went on to perform a lot of classical music, such as madrigals, in college. Even then, there was a feeling–a rush there that I wanted, and that was what pushed me back onstage. It helped me realize what my primary objective was.

Where I'm from, the environment is not prone to the arts, so I had to search for it and push myself. Every available opportunity I had to showcase my talent, I would grab it and take it.

## Making the Cut

I found out about the O-Town auditions from TV. Something inside me told me I needed to do this. Lou Pearlman was looking for singers and dancers and I definitely wanted to be one. I found out auditions were the next day, so the next morning, I got up and I went to the audition. I just went in and did my thing. The rest is history.

I think it came through to the judges that day that I had worked at training my voice. I also think there is definitely a personality issue, too. It takes a certain type of person to be able to handle what goes on in this industry, and I think they saw I would be able to do it.

What's amazing is that as many times as I wondered whether or not I was in, I knew deep in my heart I made it. I knew from that first audition that I was in, but that's not easy to accept because it's not reality. I knew in my heart that I had what it takes, and I knew I wanted it more than anything else. And all those certainties told me: I belong in this group.

The whole experience of being in O-Town changed me immensely, in positive ways, mostly. It's changed the way I look at the industry. The respect I have for other artists has gone up a hundred percent from where it was before.

Walt Disney Parks and Resorts 2000 / Mark Ashman

Judges at the audition knew Erik was O-Town material the minute he walked in the door

Tennis, anyone? Thousands of fans would love to play doubles with Erik.

Walt Disney Parks and Resorts 2000/Mark Ashman

## *Living in a Fishbowl*

I tell all the guys this: You know how those fishbowls are convex? Everything the fish does inside looks bigger than it is. So every little word, every little attitude, every little discrepancy, and every little doubt gets blown up. Every little emotion is magnified. This was our lives for a while.

I also feel that the cameras show only one aspect of a person's personality and people judge you on that one personality trait. I think the show sometimes depicted me as having an attitude, but they didn't show how I joke around most of the time. They don't show the total story.

There are a lot of negatives to living like that, but I couldn't dwell on those negatives, because I would go crazy. It was especially difficult for me because I am an only child and I crave my solitude. So I had to focus on the positives and take it as a learning experience.

*What's amazing is that as many times as I wondered whether or not I was in, I knew deep in my heart I made it.*

## *Fame*

It's weird, because I took on this whole venture because I wanted to be in a music group, but I'm noticed on the street because of the TV show. I never really thought of myself as a TV personality. But by the same token, I love attention, and now I have it. But being famous is still weird to get accustomed to.

Seeing fans screaming for us is the greatest feeling in the world. It really pumps me up. I can see how it's easy to get carried away by that, but to keep my feet on the ground I look to my friends and the other guys in the group. They're quick to let me know if I'm getting cocky or if I'm getting ahead of myself. *Real* quick.

# Erik's Mom, Micki

Erik's always talked about being a performer, so I was not surprised at all that he ended up one. What was a surprise was the audition. He just said one day; "I'm going to an audition in Orlando." And I said, "Okay, have a nice day," and pretty much left it at that. I thought, how many guys are going to be there? He's never, ever done this—what are the chances? But what did I know?

With every step, we tried to hold back our excitement. Any feelings at all, negative or positive, we tried to hold back because we didn't know what was going to happen and we wanted to be ready regardless. When he finally got to that point where he made the twenty-five, it was just incredible. It's not something that happens everyday, so we were very, very excited.

Erik and I are very close. He's my only child, so we've done a lot of things together, ever since he was a baby. And he is extremely close to us, even now. He calls us constantly to tell us everything that's new and exciting. He's very caring, and he has a really good heart. He's very sensitive, very loving, and very affectionate. He always has been.

On Mother's Day this past year it was the first time we weren't together for a holiday, and it was very hard for me. Even though he's only an hour away, we don't get to see him. I miss him because he's my best friend, really.

I want Erik to find peace, happiness, and love, and I want him to be true to Erik. He's twenty-one, a grown man, so I think he can make good decisions, but I don't want him to get lost in the celebrity of this whole thing. I want him to really focus on what it is that brought him to this point—his love for music and his desire to make people happy. I want him to take care of his gift, and not do anything to destroy it.

Ben Van Hook

## Family

I'm an only child, so I'm close with my parents. My mom raised me as a single parent for the first ten years of my life, then she got remarried. My stepfather has been a terrific role model for me, and both of them are really supportive. They knew this was what I've wanted to do my whole life and they were supportive of everything I wanted to do from the beginning. I miss them a lot right now.

*I want him to take care of his gift, and not do anything to destroy it.*
*– Erik's mom, Micki*

Behind the scenes Erik likes to joke around.

Erik is the first to admit that making a band is no pleasure cruise.

Walt Disney Parks and Resorts 2000 / Mark Ashman

## Girls, Girls, Girls

I still have so much learning and growing to do with myself. And so far, every time I thought a particular girl was for me, I was wrong. So, I've totally left that in God's hands.

I'm going to be a different person around the time I'm thinking about getting married or wholly committing to someone. So, I'm just giving myself time to grow, and when it happens, it happens.

## Is There Life After O-Town?

Ten, fifteen years from now, I still see O-Town being a big part of my life. The guys amaze me every day, and if it keeps going the way it's going, I don't really see O-Town becoming just your next act. We have so much in our heads and so much in our hearts that we want to share. And the people in this group go a lot deeper than people expect.

In the end, I want to have left a positive energy, to have been a positive spirit in this world. I was raised with strong opinions and I was raised in a very caring environment, and I feel that I can give that back, to show that to people, and have a positive effect.

*The guys amaze me every day, and if it keeps going the way it's going, I don't really see O-Town becoming just your next act.*

Walt Disney Parks and Resorts 2000 / Mark Ashman

*Erik-Michael Estrada*

Classically trained Erik hits a high note.

***Erik has a really strong passion for the music and what we're working toward.***

***– Jacob Underwood***

# On Erik

**Ashley:** Erik and I are both into ridiculous humor—Monty Python and all that kind of stuff. Lots of times we couldn't go to sleep because we'd just stay up late laughing. He is also always there for any one of us if we ever need him.

**Dan:** Erik is a very funny guy, and his voice is incredible. But he's also a little irresponsible. Sometimes he acts like the youngest. If you don't tell him what time something is scheduled, he'll forget. This doesn't mean he isn't a hard worker, though. When Erik puts his mind to something, he gets everything accomplished.

**Jacob:** Erik has a really strong passion for the music and what we're working toward. He's always late, like Ashley, but he's hilarious and he's very talented.

**Trevor:** He's very funny. We're always constantly doing skits back and forth. That's one thing we love to do. And he's very serious with his work.

**Mark Goff, vocal coach:** My relationship with Erik has changed quite a bit. I ride him pretty hard because I see such potential in him. In the beginning, I just don't think he ever understood he needed to work hard; nor do I think he has had to work hard for anything in his life. I get this sense from him that it's always been kind of good and he's been told that, so accepting criticism from a constructive angle has been very difficult. He has improved immensely, not only in his attitude but also in his ability to understand the rehearsal situation and absorb the constructive criticism and use it. He has really made an effort to apply it to what he does, and, because of this, he has made some great strides as a singer. I'm very proud of him—as an individual as well as a singer.

**Marc Piacenza, road manager:** Erik's a *New Yawka*, like me.

**Tyjuan Jones, choreographer:** Erik is one of the most vocally talented people I've met in a long time, and he has a natural ability to be onstage. He had some attitude problems in the beginning, which I don't think he saw as problems, because he saw them as simply the way he is. He's had to learn to adapt, and he has adapted very well. He has come a long way adjusting to dealing with everyone, and his talent is really, really broad.

**Raymond Del Barrio, choreographer:** Erik is talented, but my personal experience of Erik was that he doesn't know how to handle authority. He was young, understandably. He might have grown out of it now.

**Erik on Erik:** I think my voice is a strong contribution to the group. I don't stop at one style and I can manipulate my voice to do anything. It may seem unorthodox, but it's just the way I've trained myself to be, and that's probably the biggest plus I bring to O-Town.

# ASHLEY

Ben Van Hook

©2000 ABC, Inc / Kevin Kolczynski

# Fast Facts

**Birthdate:** August 1, 1981
**Sign:** Leo
**Hometown:** Redding, CA
**Family:** mom, Paula; dad, Ronald; brother Taylor, thirty-four; sisters Annie, twenty-one; and Emily, nineteen
**Favorite group:** Third Eye Blind
**Favorite book:** *Illusions* by Richard Bach
**Favorite TV show:** *Friends*
**Favorite movie:** *The Matrix*
**Favorite actor:** Robert De Niro
**Favorite actress:** Susan Sarandon
**Favorite food:** cold cereal
**Favorite thing to do when he's not working:** go to the movies
**What's in his Walkman:** Third Eye Blind
**Professional role model:** Harrison Ford

# Ashley Parker Angel

Did you ever wonder where Sega and Playstation get the voices for their CD games? From voice actors. Being a voice actor for those games was my first professional "acting" job. But while I loved acting, music was always at the forefront of what I wanted to do.

From a very young age I remember watching Michael Jackson tapes and thinking he was the most incredible performer I had ever seen. There was something about his music and something about his stage presence that was so captivating. This was when I first knew a career in music was for me.

I had been playing piano since I was four because my mom was a piano teacher, and I taught myself how to play guitar when I was twelve. Then I started practic-

Ben Van Hook

**The other guys view young Ashley as the group's little brother.**

ing singing while I was playing guitar. Though I had some vocal lessons while I was in a play, I basically taught myself how to sing.

When I auditioned for O-Town, I was working a part-time job, going to school part-time, and taking acting classes. Through the classes, I used to get something called a "breakdown"–it's a daily fax of all the different parts that casting agents are looking for. It's not often that you see an audition for a musical group, so it was my lucky break that the O-Town audition was on there. If it hadn't been a TV show, I don't think I would have ever found out about it. The minute I decided to go on that audition, my life changed.

## Making the Cut

I think the judges saw I had all the skills: I could dance, I could sing, I could play guitar. But I think they wanted engaging personalities, too. They needed people with enough character to make a great television show. I think they saw potential in me, plus a drive and a hunger. I was willing to shoot above and beyond everybody's expectations.

This is what I've wanted to do my entire life. And now that I'm here, I'm not going to let anything stop me from going as far as I want to go. And that goes for the rest of the guys, too. We're doing it as a team.

If I didn't make it, I would probably be doing the same thing I was before, which was writing music, singing, playing guitar and piano, doing theater. Somehow I think I would have eventually hit it in acting or music.

## *Living in a Fishbowl*

We're the first band that has had everything documented from the start. The viewers go through all of our triumphs and challenges with us, and, because of this, they're more connected to us since they watched it all happen from the beginning.

We watch the episodes every Friday night as they come out, and the hardest thing for me to watch, personally, was when I went home and talked to my dad. I relived some of that pain all over again, even though it's better between us now.

Each week we'd have to sit down and have an interview with the camera, just one-on-one. For me, a lot of healing went on during that time, because I could get things off my chest. They'd see little things and bring them out and discuss them openly, so it helped me with a lot of things.

It helped me grow, and the whole experience helped me learn a lot about myself. I learned about how I interact with a group, the way I handle stress, and the way I handle pressure. Because of these experiences I think I'm a lot more responsible.

Walt Disney Parks and Resorts 2000 / Mark Ashman

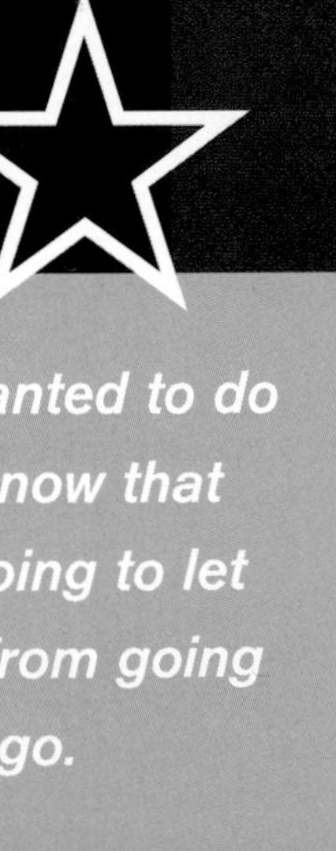

*This is what I've wanted to do my entire life. And now that I'm here, I'm not going to let anything stop me from going as far as I want to go.*

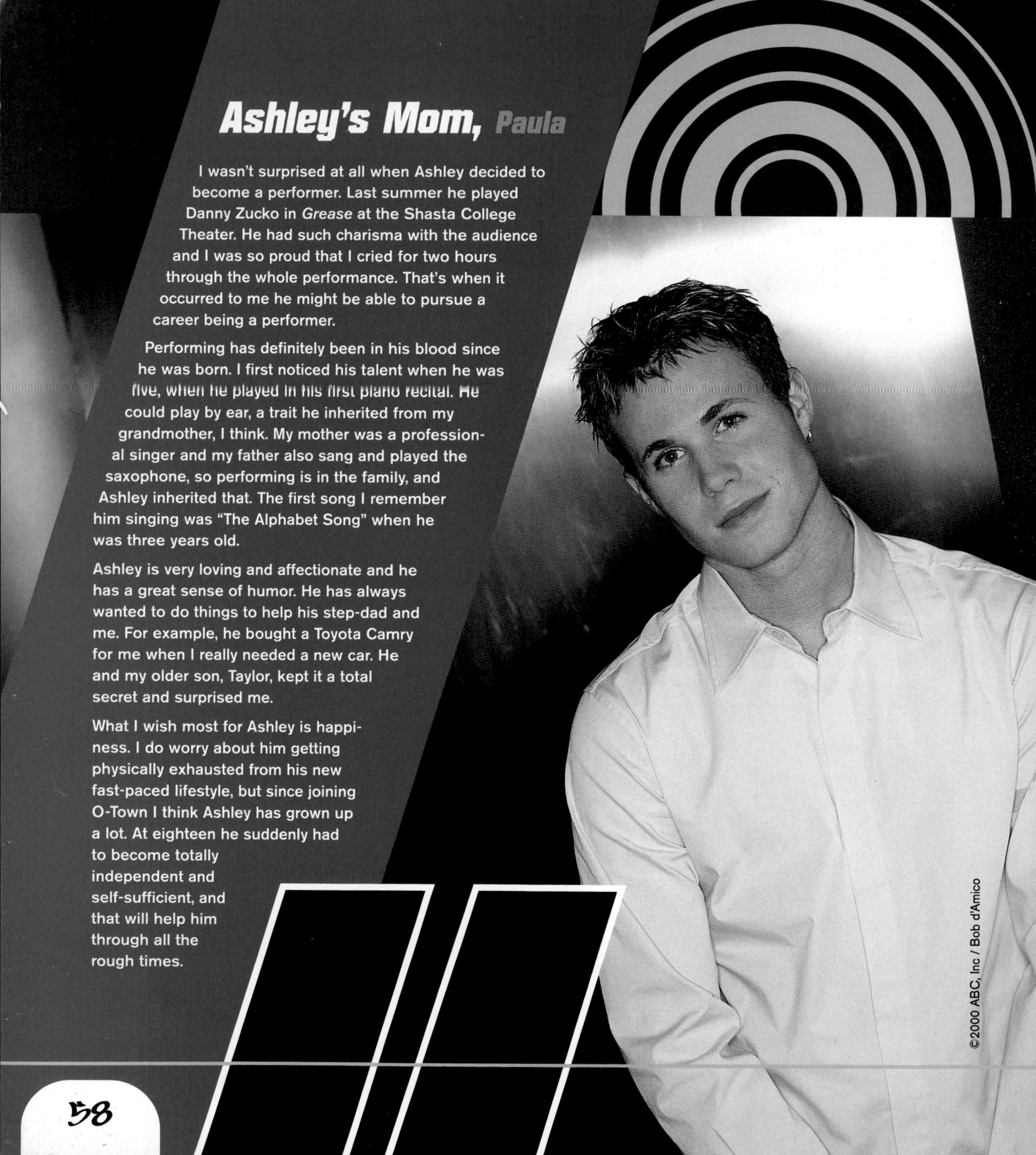

## Ashley's Mom, Paula

I wasn't surprised at all when Ashley decided to become a performer. Last summer he played Danny Zucko in *Grease* at the Shasta College Theater. He had such charisma with the audience and I was so proud that I cried for two hours through the whole performance. That's when it occurred to me he might be able to pursue a career being a performer.

Performing has definitely been in his blood since he was born. I first noticed his talent when he was five, when he played in his first piano recital. He could play by ear, a trait he inherited from my grandmother, I think. My mother was a professional singer and my father also sang and played the saxophone, so performing is in the family, and Ashley inherited that. The first song I remember him singing was "The Alphabet Song" when he was three years old.

Ashley is very loving and affectionate and he has a great sense of humor. He has always wanted to do things to help his step-dad and me. For example, he bought a Toyota Camry for me when I really needed a new car. He and my older son, Taylor, kept it a total secret and surprised me.

What I wish most for Ashley is happiness. I do worry about him getting physically exhausted from his new fast-paced lifestyle, but since joining O-Town I think Ashley has grown up a lot. At eighteen he suddenly had to become totally independent and self-sufficient, and that will help him through all the rough times.

*It's the coolest thing in the world to have people recognize you from the show, and say, "Hey—you're from Making the Band! That's such a cool show!"*

## Fame

You're never quite ready to know what it's like to walk down the street and have people notice you and recognize you until it actually happens. And I absolutely love it! It's the coolest thing in the world to have people recognize you from the show, and say, "Hey—you're from *Making the Band*! That's such a cool show!"

When we performed in Georgia, I remember looking at this girl and she was crying and screaming. I had always seen that in concert videos for other bands, but this time it was for me, and it was the most exhilarating feeling ever! It put me totally in tune with the song I was singing and made me really feel the music.

When we were in Germany, these girls drove nine hours—the whole day—just to see us. They hung around our hotel in the lobby until it closed, and they slept in their car at night. And it's cold in Germany at night! We felt bad because the next morning they saw us only for about ten, twenty minutes, and then we had to go record. The craziest thing is they had never heard any of our music, and they had never seen our show, yet they were the most devoted fans in the world.

My family is there to help keep me grounded with all of the fuss, but it is hard not being able to talk with them and my friends because of the time constraints. I'd hate for them to think I hit the big time and I'm forgetting all about them, so I always try to make an extra effort to tell people, "Hey, I'm thinking about you."

## Family

The worst part of being in O-Town is being away from home and not being able to see my family. They miss me a lot, and I miss them, so whenever I go home, I try to see all the family I can.

As more and more people come up to my dad and say, "We're really proud of Ashley," I think he realizes this experience is not such a bad thing. But I don't think he will ever support me 100 percent in doing this, just because he has to stand up for what he believes in, too, and he believes me being so far away from home and being in the entertainment industry will open up a lot of temptations.

But as time goes on, our relationship gets better. Our relationship has never been bad, it's just we have never really shared the same interest in performing. We've only really butted heads on this one issue. And we have always talked—we still talk on the phone when I call home. But I just can't say, "Hey, Dad, we're performing at House of Blues!" I don't talk to him about things like that.

My mom is my number one fan. For Mother's Day, I bought her a car. She had the same car forever and ever, and me and my brother both went in and we bought her a new one. It was so awesome, because my mom is so awesome. I look up to her so much. She's the strongest, most well-rounded person, and she's the best mom ever. I know everyone says that about his or her mom, but my mom really is.

Going solo: Ashley misses having a girlfriend, but he feels he's too busy to be a good boyfriend right now.

Walt Disney Parks and Resorts 2000 / Mark Ashman

**Sent from heaven: thousands of girls want to be Ashley's angel.**

## Girls, Girls, Girls

Having a long-distance relationship was no fun. Things started getting really tough between my girlfriend, Shelli, and me because she was used to me having so much time with her, and suddenly I was in Florida and she was in California.

I finally told her that I thought we should take time apart, and we decided to break up, but still talk to each other. I thought it would be good to have things be a lot less committed because while trying to deal with everything that was happening with the group it was hard for me to be the boyfriend I wanted to be. And I'd always thought of myself as a really good boyfriend up until then.

The only reason I wanted to take a break was not to meet a lot of different girls but because I knew that if I stayed with Shelli, she'd continue to be unhappy. I started to feel responsible for her unhappiness, and her happiness is important to me. She deserves so much because she's such an incredible person–she's smart, she's beautiful, she's funny, she's awesome, and I have a lot of respect for her.

I miss Shelli a lot, but I've always thought that if it's meant to be, it's meant to be. Right now in my life I have to focus so much on this project that it would be hard for me to be a good boyfriend to anyone.

## Is There Life After O-Town?

I think we have a lot of time together as O-Town, but when it's all over, I'm definitely going to go back into acting. Growing up, I always knew I would either go into music or acting, and now that I'm pursuing music, I know that later my path will be acting.

*Growing up, I always knew I would either go into music or acting, and now that I'm pursuing music, I know that later my path will be acting.*

***Ashley Parker Angel***

# On Ashley

**Erik:** Ashley is a very sweet individual. He's young and he has a lot to learn, but he is going to be a very, very powerful musician—more than any of us expect.

**Dan:** He's a very funny guy, and very talented as well. He's not the most responsible person, though. He's late every once in a while, and if he had to pay bills on his own, he probably wouldn't. But he's very smart and dedicated to what he wants to do.

**Jacob:** He's the little brother of all of us. He's a lot like my little brother back home. They both have the same attitude—that everything will always work out.

**Trevor:** Ashley is the baby. He's the one who is always asking the questions. But he's very smart and wise for an eighteen-year-old.

**Tyjuan Jones, choreographer:** Ashley is a great musician. He's very into the mellow side of the singing and performing aspect and I think that's going to contribute to the softer, sensitive, emotional side of the group.

**Mark Goff, vocal coach:** Professionally, he has a lot of challenges ahead of him in terms of being consistent. I had a hard time keeping his attention focused where it needed to be focused. Personally, he's an outstanding individual, and he's a wonderful person.

**Marc Piacenza, road manager:** He's very humble. He knows what he wants and he knows how to achieve his goals, which makes him a very special member of the group.

**Raymond Del Barrio, choreographer:** His last name is Angel. That says it all: He's an angel, a really good kid, and really focused and genuine.

**Ashley on Ashley:** I'm kind of the middleman in the group. I'm not really opinionated, and I'm not really shy, so whenever there's a debate I think I'm the compromiser. I also think the guys feel they can confide in me.

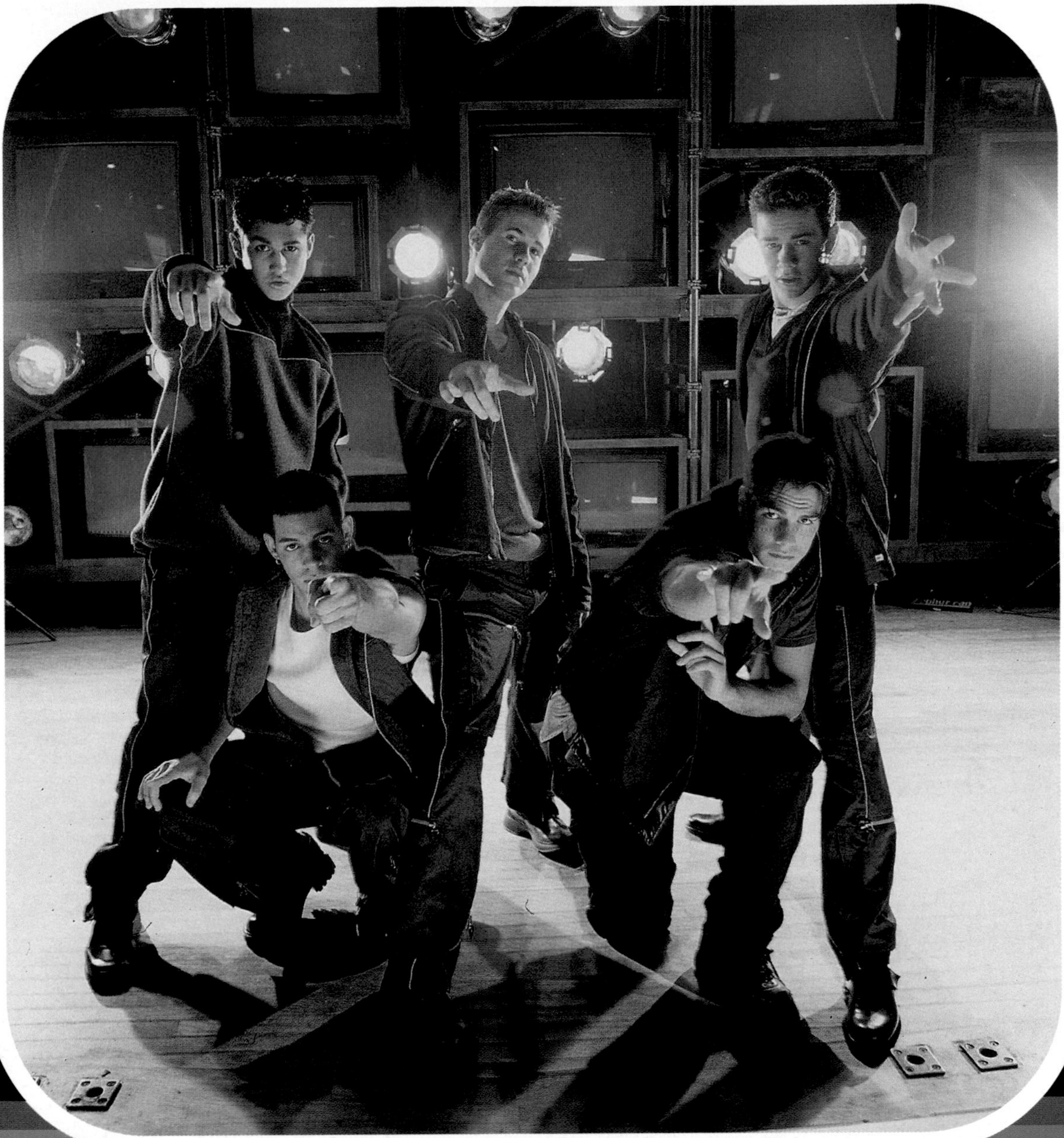

©2000 ABC, Inc / Marina Chavez

*He's a very funny guy, and very talented as well.*
*– Dan Miller*

# JACOB

Ben Van Hook

©2000 ABC, Inc / Kevin Kolczynski

# Jacob Underwood

## Fast Facts

**Birthdate:** April 25, 1980

**Sign:** Taurus

**Hometown:** El Cajon, CA

**Family:** mom, Mechele; dad, Steve; brother Bryan, eighteen; sister Danielle, fourteen

**Favorite bands:** Korn, Tool, and Creed

**Favorite book:** The Bible

**Favorite TV show:** *Friends*

**Favorite movie:** Love too many to pick one!

**Favorite actor:** Mel Gibson, Edward Norton

**Favorite actress:** don't have one

**Favorite thing to do when he's not working:** playing guitar or creating anything

**Favorite food:** cereal

**What's in his Walkman:** Eminem

**Professional role model:** Michael Jackson

Everything in my life seemed to lead to O-Town. I was always drawn to music, and I always strove to be the best at whatever I became involved in. For example, I started wrestling in preschool. By the time I was in fourth grade, I was state champion in California and Arizona. But in the process I tore all my ligaments, so I couldn't play sports anymore. So right after that, in the fifth grade, I got into the theater and music.

I didn't really take it seriously, though, until sophomore year of high school, when I switched schools to go to one with better ensembles. The only classes I paid attention to in high school were the music theory classes. It was tough for me to concentrate on anything else because I looked at other subjects as a waste of time. I've always been focused like that.

For the last three years I was in a hard-rock band trying to make it in San Diego. I don't have any regrets about leaving that scene behind, because I am sure it will be back for me. Somehow, I'll get into it again.

Igor Stravinsky, the great composer, once said that to become great yourself, you have to first follow the people that came before you. So I looked to people like Michael Jackson. I want to do what Michael did to James Brown—taking what the greats did before you and bringing it to the next level.

## Making the Cut

A friend of my dad told me about the O-Town audition. He was making fun of me because I was into hard rock, and everybody was always telling me that I'm perfect for a boy band. They would tell me that I can sing and dance and that I had a pretty face, teasingly. So, when my dad's friend first mentioned the audition, I didn't want to go. But then one of my friends stepped in. He filled out the form for me and sent everything in. Then I got a callback from what he gave them, and I just kept moving on. I guess my dad's friend was right—that I had the look, the charisma, and talent they were looking for.

Jacob says that all roads led him to O-Town.

Walt Disney Parks and Resorts 2000 / Mark Ashman

Walt Disney Parks and Resorts 2000 / Mark Ashman

*I was always drawn to music, and I always strove to be the best at whatever I became involved in.*

## *Living in a Fishbowl*

It's hard to be scrutinized all the time. It's harder to be picked on by people like Rosie O'Donnell. She says that I yelled at Ikaika, and Ikaika and I are actually really good friends now! They showed me on the show saying that if he's in the group, then I'm leaving. Everybody else in the group felt that way, too, but they only showed me saying it. The editors give a great overview of what happened, but they can't show everything. They shoot over two hundred hours a week, and they only show about twenty minutes of it. So, it irritates me that Rosie doesn't know the whole truth. What can I do? I guess I have to just sit back and let her believe what she wants to believe.

It was hard to get used to the cameras at first. For the first two weeks it was a total invasion of privacy, but we all opened up after that and treated them like they were flies on the wall. By the end, though, we were glad we didn't have to wear the mike packs anymore.

New Year's Eve was hard to watch again. I still think that Marc, our road manager, was wrong about us not being able to be ourselves now because we are in a group. I think the only reason why people can't be themselves is because they're afraid that somebody's not going to agree with them, and that they might lose their fan base or something. I'm not going to be afraid to stand up for what I believe in because I'm going to lose fans or money over it. It's just a difference of opinion I have. And every person has an opinion and shouldn't be afraid to speak it.

## Jacob's Mom, Mechele:

Jacob was so driven to become a musician, so I'm not surprised at all by his success. He was driving me crazy with all of his creative energy, so I said to him, "You'd better move to L.A.!"

Jacob always has something going. He's a type-A personality, with tons of energy, and a stubbornness to him, which makes him a really strong leader. He's not in the business just to be famous and sit around and have fun and games. He's in it to impact people.

I first found out about Jacob's talent when he was in fifth grade and he was cast in a Christmas production. During auditions, people walked up to me and asked, "Do you know that your son can sing?" But I didn't really think much of it until the actual show when he sang into a microphone and blew the whole church away. I had tears just rolling down my eyes. He sang "My Father Is a King." From there on, every time he sang, no matter where it was, people would approach him and tell him that he's going to make it big someday.

His success has affected his family in the sense that we're very strong Christians, and we're not real happy with the way the TV end of it is coming out. Personally, I'm very proud of Jacob and all the young men on how they're handling this. But it has been hard, because people all have their comments, don't they? Sometimes it's real hard on me, but it brings me to prayer. Jacob is going to make mistakes, and it's going to be hard, but he was raised in a good, strong home and he's twenty years old. It's also hard for a mom to sit back and watch her son go through the pressures of it all.

He's got a peace about him now that he is musically on his way, and I see a lot of happiness in him now because he had a goal that was set, and he reached it. My biggest wish is for Jacob to continue walking in God's truth. My biggest worry is that he might get away from God's word and that his heart will become a little hard. I don't want him to be lost without God.

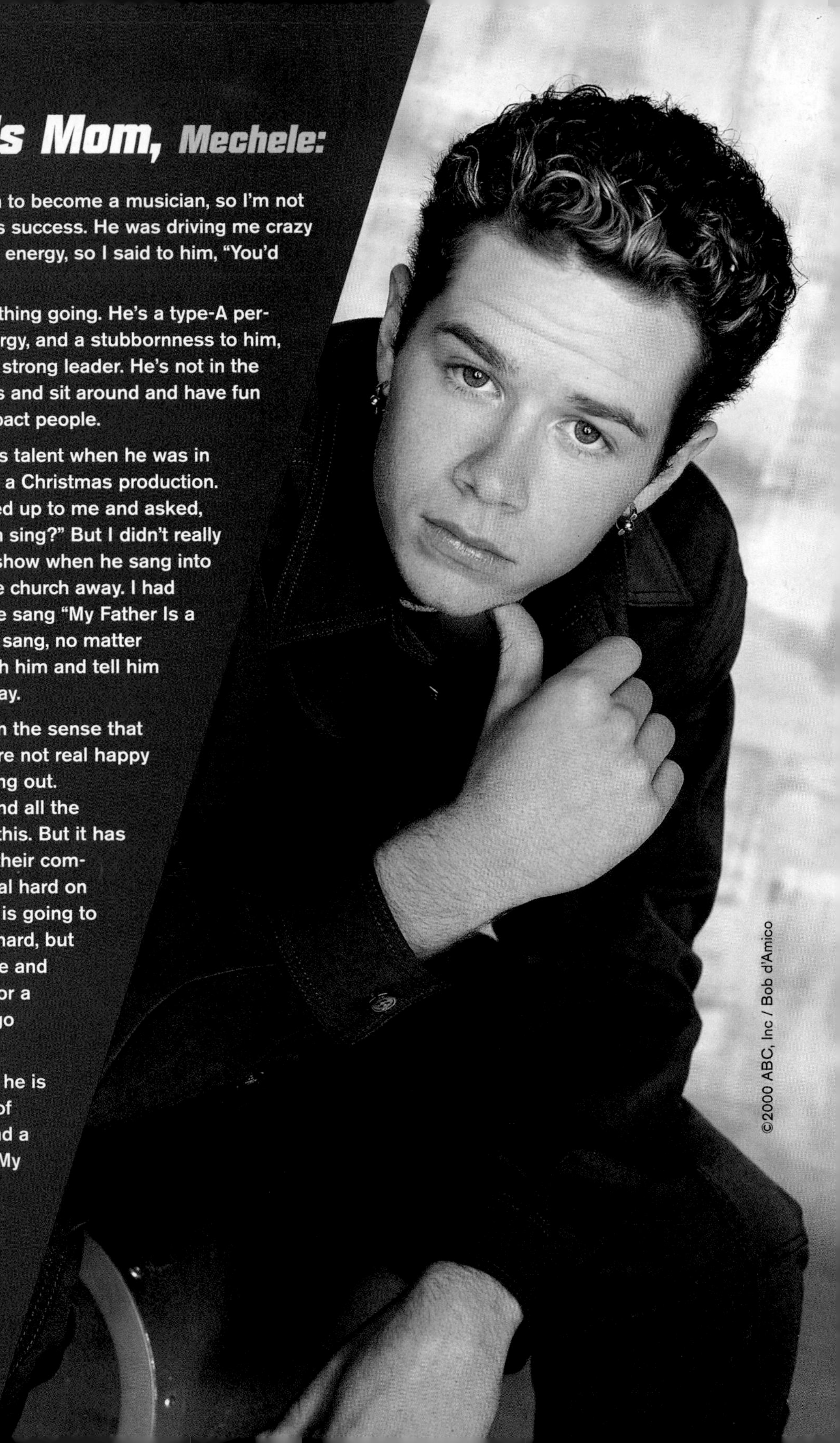

## Fame

I always wanted to be in the spotlight in the music scene. And I knew it was going to happen when I was young, but this quick? Honestly, the whole thing is a blessing. I once only dreamed about changing music and impacting the music world, let alone having my own TV show at the same time. The whole thing is bigger than a dream come true.

It's great to be able to make an impact on the timeline of music. I want people to want to listen to me, and the bigger I am, the more people will listen to what I have to say. When all eyes are on me, I want to make sure they stay there, so I want to give them something to see. It challenges me to come up with different things for people to watch me for.

I like being recognized, because I look at it as people respecting what I'm doing and they're happy for me. I love that part of it but I think it's scary at some points, because I always have to watch how I act. For example, if I get mad or frustrated with somebody, even though if I have a legitimate argument, then that person might become really mad and start spreading rumors or something. I could end up with this big, horrible rep just because I had a bad day, which everybody has. So fame has its down side, too.

## Family

I have a really close family. Although I have just one brother and one sister, I have forty-six cousins, and thirty-eight of them lived within twenty minutes of my house, so we all grew up close to each other. My family has given me a great relationship with God, which helps me keep it real, and I believe very strongly in God and having a good family life.



*It's great to be able to make an impact on the timeline of music.*

**A rare time-out for hardworking Jacob and the guys.**

## *Girls, Girls, Girls*

I think the show focused a lot on our relationships with girls, and that was a reminder for me of past mistakes. Every experience with girls on the show with us—not one of them works out! If things didn't happen on the show, they happened after the show—bad breakups, dates, and such. We all had bad experiences with girls. And now when I see the show it just reminds me of the mistakes I made with girls.

Right now the most important girl in my life is my longest-lasting friend—but we're not dating. We are just going on with our lives, but we are very connected.

The girl I settle down with will be a hometown girl—a San Diego girl. She'll enjoy going to the beach, have a great sense of humor, take pleasure in the arts, and have a strong faith in God.

Jacob takes the business of music seriously.

## Is There Life After O-Town?

I have dreams and plans of where I want to be at that point, but I don't want to say anything. I'll just let you wait to see what's going to happen.

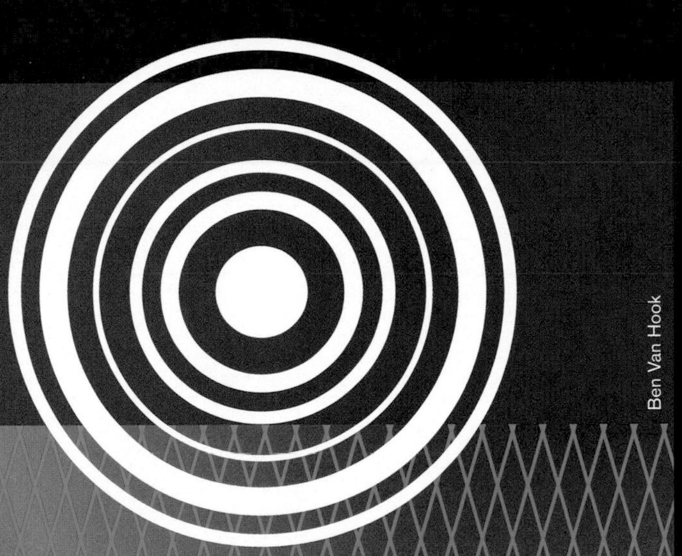

Ben Van Hook

*The girl I settle down with will be a hometown girl—a San Diego girl.*

Jacob Underwood

Walt Disney Parks and Resorts 2000 / Mark Ashman

*Jacob is the all-around musician of the group.... We always ask for his advice, musically or in terms of our careers.*

*– Trevor*

# On Jacob

**Ashley:** I saw Jacob in the Arizona Airport terminal, and I didn't know who he was, but I looked at him and I thought: *I bet he's flying with me to Orlando. I bet he is!* He had that look about him. And we both got on the same plane together, and then I didn't actually talk to him until we both got off. He said the same thing about me. He's a really great singer and dancer and I really respect his level of dedication. He wants this really bad, and he's really dedicated.

**Dan:** Jacob is all about the business. He is very, very talented in everything, but when it comes to the business aspect, he's very knowledgeable. He's cautious of his career, and anything or anybody that gets in the way is going to get a piece of Jacob's mind. As talented as he is, the boy takes his stuff seriously, and he knows what he's doing.

**Erik:** Jacob's definitely a brother to me. We bond on a certain level that's very difficult to explain. It's almost like we've known each other our whole lives. I went to his house once and his mom told me that when Jacob was little he used to sing a song from this Christian tape called "Aunt Sylvania." I couldn't believe it because I used to sing it all through my childhood, just like Jacob. It's something that you can only get in certain places, like Christian bookstores. And he had it. There's been of bunch of little coincidences like that with the two of us.

**Trevor:** Jacob is the all-around musician of the group. He's the one I think everybody looks up to when they have a question about something. We always ask for his advice, musically or in terms of our careers.

**Mark Goff, vocal coach:** Jacob has grown. His range has improved; his stamina has improved. I think he was pretty strong-headed and a little narrow-minded early on, but I think he also has grown tremendously as an individual, and he's learning to communicate in a working environment.

**Marc Piacenza, road manager:** Talent just oozes out of Jacob's pores. He knows what he wants out of this business, and he has the perfect attitude.

**Tyjuan Jones, choreographer:** Jacob is what I call the 100 percent overall entertainer. He is a fabulous dancer, a wonderful singer, and just has a great personality. He's the quiet one of the group, not that he's quiet, but he's the one who's reserved and laid-back. He's definitely an artist.

**Raymond Del Barrio, choreographer:** Jacob is brilliant. He's a trouper, and was really in there to work, and actually got really down on the guys when they were not working.

**Jacob on Jacob:** I see myself as a person who stands up very strongly for things I believe musically and businesswise. I've been doing this a lot longer than anybody, and I'm the only person in the group that wasn't in college at the time—right out of high school I played music and that was my plan. So I knew what it was like to work all day long at a full-time job and then rehearse, practice, and write songs at night. So I bring to the group a realization of how it is in the real music world.

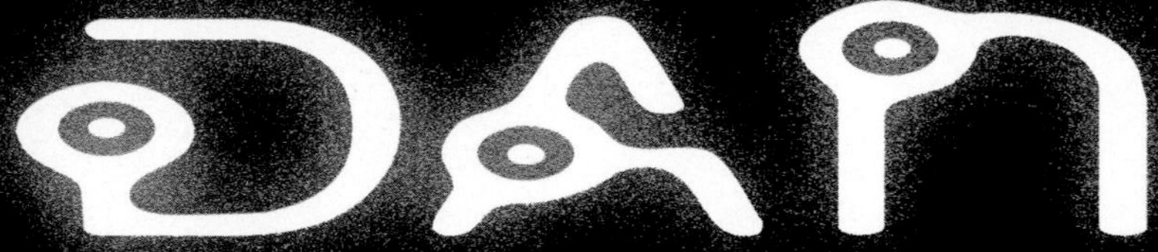

Ben Van Hook

Ben Van Hook

# FAST FACTS

**Birthdate:** September 4, 1980

**Sign:** Virgo

**Hometown:** Twinsburg, OH

**Family:** mom, Angela; dad, Mark; brothers Adam, seventeen; and Kevin, nine; sister Allison, fourteen

**Favorite band:** Boyz II Men

**Favorite book:** Charlotte's Web by E.B. White

**Favorite TV show:** Whose Line Is It Anyway?

**Favorite movie:** Dumb and Dumber

**Favorite actor:** Jim Carrey

**Favorite actress:** Meg Ryan

**Favorite thing to do when he's not working:** Sit in front of the TV in boxer shorts

**Favorite food:** Chicken parmesan

**What's in his Walkman:** D'angelo

**Professional role model:** Michael Jordan

# Dan Miller

O experienced the rejection of this whole process at first, so I think I bring another dimension to this group. I knew what it felt like to go home, to go back to where I came from with just the memories of having my shot.

It was always a dream of mine to be a performer but I never had enough confidence in my talents, knowing it is such a tough industry to break into. I thought I could be a producer or something–somebody behind the scenes–something more realistic to break into. I really wanted to be onstage, but I just thought it would never happen. Only a couple of people get lucky. I guess I finally got lucky.

My experience prior to O-Town was based on putting on a lot of little shows for my family–I used to sing and dance everywhere from the backyard to the dinner table

New kid on the block Dan fit in with O-Town right away.

to my garage. I was never really taught to dance. One day one of my neighbors wanted to do a talent show, so I decided that I would dance with him. From there, I just started picking up on things. When the school dances came around, that was my time to shine—that's where I honed my dance skills.

In high school I was in a show choir. I did that for four years. We were a very good choir—we competed nationally and did very well. That's where I learned a lot about performance.

Before the O-Town auditions, I was going to school at the University of Cincinnati, majoring in electronic media, and I was completely happy there, just living my life and not expecting anything big to happen.

Little did I know.

## Making the Cut

I was online one day and I was looking for information on *The Real World,* and there was a link that said: "Do you want to be on TV?" And I was, like, sure! So I clicked it and it gave me audition information for O-Town. I sent in a tape, and I never got a call back. But I noticed the auditions in Nashville were open for everybody, so I decided to go anyway. The day before I was leaving, I got a call asking me to come. It was a good thing I made plans to go!

I couldn't believe it when I actually made the top twenty-five, and I wasn't crushed when I didn't make the eight. I felt in my heart that something better was going to come out of it. There were too many people involved, too many different people looking for too many different things for me to get upset that I didn't get picked.

No one was more surprised than I was when I got the call to replace Ikaika. It was difficult to step into a new group of people, a group that had already formed a bond. My challenge wasn't so much worrying about the dancing and singing, which is, I think, what the guys worried about when they brought me in. They were worrying if I could pick up what they had done in so short a time. My main concern and my biggest challenge was to bond with these guys and make sure that I fit in. It was important for me to make sure I liked the guys and they liked me and our personalities matched. I thought the best way to fit in was to just be myself, but it was also very hard, because at the same time I was concerned about that, we had tons of other stuff to do. Luckily, the guys took me in with open arms and it's been nothing but smooth since.

## Living in a Fishbowl

We have to remember it's because of the cameras we're in the position we're in. Because of the cameras, I was in a group for two weeks, and the next thing I knew we were auditioning for record companies and putting on shows. A "normal" group would never dream of performing after two weeks of being together. We try to keep making big leaps and strides and always keep improving, whether the cameras are there or not. Because if the cameras aren't there, there's going be a crowd anyway—whether it be record company people, choreographers, whoever. There's always somebody watching.

It does take a load off our shoulders to have the cameras off, though. We have talked to our choreographers and vocal coach since then, and it was hard for them to say some things at times, too. With the cameras off, we've had some times where people have been able to be completely and totally honest with each other where there were times when they felt a little weird before.

Walt Disney Parks and Resorts 2000 / Mark Ashman

Dan has been smiling ever since the guys picked him to replace Ikaika.

*My main concern and my biggest challenge was to bond with these guys and make sure that I fit in.*

*Dan Miller*

# Dan's Mom, Angela

Danny is at his happiest when he is singing and dancing. My husband and I feel that if there's something you love to do and you have a chance to make a living at it—even if only for a while—you're pretty lucky to be able to do it, so we are really happy things worked out for him.

He has been dancing in particular ever since he was born. He was always really drawn to the Mickey Mouse Club and Kids Incorporated and all those shows with dancing. And as he started to get older he would sing around the house. When he was in sixth or seventh grade I would hear him singing on the phone, and it turned out girls that knew him from school were calling him. They had heard him sing in music class, and they would call and say, "Sing to us!"

Danny is a great kid. He's hardworking, he's dedicated, he's loyal, he's very principled. He's well liked and he's well respected. I think you would really have to look hard to find people who know Danny and don't respect him, because he is very honest, he says what he feels, and he works hard at everything he does. He is a good friend to his friends. He's a good son. He's a good brother. He's a good boyfriend to his girlfriends. He's an all-around good guy. We're very proud of him.

It's hard with him gone. He was in college and away from home already, but we thought we had a few more years of him being here for the summer, and for holidays and vacations. We miss him a lot.

I sometimes worry that he won't be treated well by the people that he works with. Five young guys with no real experience in the music business—that's a scary thing. But Danny's doing what he always wanted, and that will bring him happiness and success.

*With the cameras off, we've had some times where people have been able to be completely and totally honest with each other.*

Walt Disney Parks and Resorts 2000 / Mark Ashman

## Fame

It was so hard in the beginning when the show was starting to take off, and it wasn't revealed yet that Ikaika had quit. So I was a secret for a while, a mystery man. The original eight would be doing promotions and things and I wouldn't be a part of it—*that* would be tough sometimes.

Before it was revealed I was the fifth member, we'd be in a mall and the other guys would get recognized, and a little girl would hand me her camera and say, "Can you take our picture?" Stuff like that would happen all the time.

Another time we were in the airport and an all-girls' school going on vacation together recognized us. There were about sixty girls and this one girl asked me flat out: "Are you in the group, too?" I was, but at the time I couldn't tell her. I said, "You just have to watch the show." That was my only response to everything: "Just watch the show—you might see me again!" But I knew that eventually my time would come.

## Family

My family is supersupportive. And they were especially great when I was a secret and they couldn't tell anyone. People would ask, "So, how's Dan?" And they weren't able to say "He's great! He's going to be on TV later this summer!" They would just say, "Well, he's fine." That was really hard for them, because I'm sure they would have loved to have told everybody in town!

## Girls, Girls, Girls

I definitely miss having a lady friend to hang out with. Ever since I got here, most of the people I hang out with are guys. I miss having a woman's point of view on some things.

My girlfriend, Cindy, and I both want to do a lot of things, and we don't want to get in the way of each other. So we have an open relationship—it's perfect for both of us. We don't necessarily have to talk to each other every day or every other day, because we know we're both busy. Some girlfriends would get upset if they couldn't talk to their boyfriend or see him, but Cindy's okay with that. We have a relationship where we're not completely tied down because we know a lot of things can happen through this whole situation. People change and situations change. So we're both very mature about it and we have a good hold on what's going on.

It's hard to say if our relationship will last because this is the hardest thing we've ever had to go through. It's been on the ropes at times. We'd like to think that we can push through it, but, again, it's hard to tell. We have a strong relationship, but this is a really tough time now.

## Is There Life After O-Town?

I think we're going to keep O-Town going for as long as we can. As long as we put out good records and people buy our music, we're going to go on. After O-Town, I would like to get into producing, and get into the inside of the business.

**Dan adds maturity and hot dance moves to the O-Town mix.**

Walt Disney Parks and Resorts 2000 / Mark Ashman

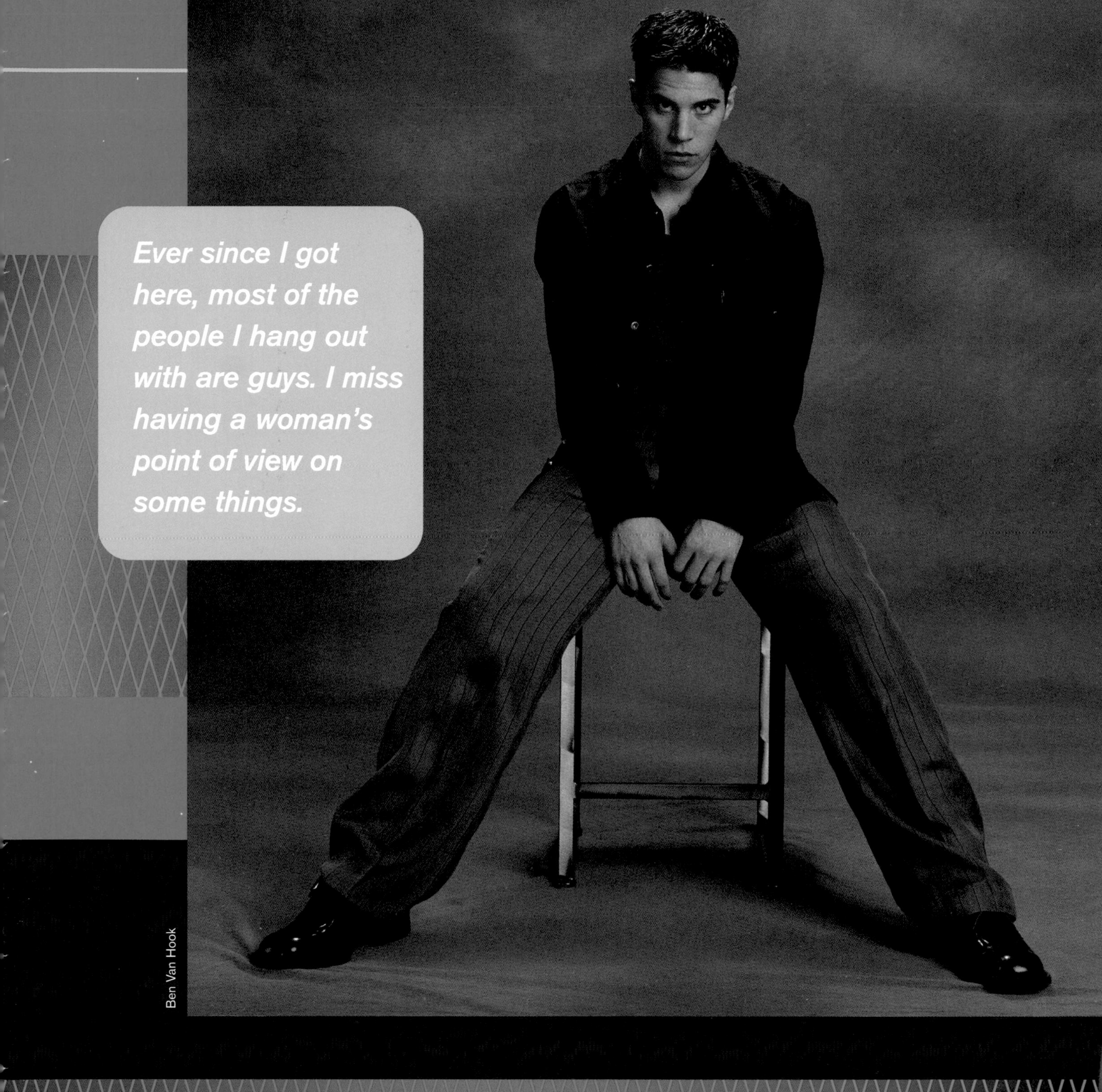
*Ever since I got here, most of the people I hang out with are guys. I miss having a woman's point of view on some things.*
Ben Van Hook

# On Dan

***Ashley:*** We were all really happy when Dan joined the group. He came and he fit in perfectly. Within four days, we were in Germany, recording, and within two weeks performing together.

***Erik:*** Dan is a blessing sent from God. He came in and learned everything when we needed him to. And he also brings a specific timbre to the group—a tonality in his voice that just fills in perfectly with Jacob and me.

***Jacob:*** Dan's the only responsible one in the group. If it weren't for him, we'd be evicted from our apartment in the first month! He pays all the bills, and Dan knows that if he doesn't take care of it, it won't happen.

***Trevor:*** Dan is Mr. Put Us On the Ball. He's also Mr. Punctuality. He's always telling us, "You can't be late for this. You can't be late for that." He also has a tremendous amount of energy onstage.

***Mark Goff, vocal coach:*** Vocally, Dan gave me no grief. He's really self-motivated and he knows what's necessary to get the job done. I felt bad for him coming into that situation because we had developed some momentum; however, the rest of the guys crashed all at the same time, and he was still fresh.

***Marc Piacenza, road manager:*** Dan is Mini-Me! Dan is the hard-time, down-to-earth person that keeps everybody in line and on time. He's very efficient.

***Tyjuan Jones, choreographer:*** Dan is definitely the sergeant of the group. He's the one who always wants to get rehearsals started, and he's the one who always wants to keep rehearsing and make sure everything is right.

***Dan on Dan:*** I think I bring leadership and a certain maturity level to the group. I'm a very get-things-done-on-time kind of person. I like for everything I'm doing to be very organized, whereas the rest of the guys in the group are a little . . . lack-adaisical in those areas.

Walt Disney Parks and Resorts 2000 / Mark Ashman

Circular photos: ©2000 ABC, Inc / Bob d'Amico; except Dan Miller photo by Walt Disney Parks and Resorts 2000 / Mark Ashman

Ben Van Hook

*Dan is a blessing sent from God. He came in and learned everything when we needed him to.*

*– Erik*

K.M. Squires is the author of the *New York Times* bestsellers *'N SYNC: The Official Book,* and *98 Degrees: The Official Book*. She contributes to magazines and is currently at work on a novel. She lives in Manhattan with her husband, Ronnie.